REVOLUTION AND TRADITION IN

# modern american art

# REVOLUTION AND TRADITION IN

# modern american art

JOHN I. H. BAUR

**FREDERICK A. PRAEGER,** *Publishers*
New York · Washington · London

FREDERICK A. PRAEGER, PUBLISHERS
111 Fourth Avenue, New York, N.Y. 10003, U.S.A.
77–79 Charlotte Street, London W.1, England

Published in the United States of America in 1967
by Frederick A. Praeger, Inc., Publishers

© 1951 by the President and Fellows of Harvard College
Introduction © 1967 by John I. H. Baur

Library of Congress Catalog Card Number: 67-27417

The original clothbound edition of this book was
published in 1951 by the Harvard University Press,
Cambridge, Mass.

Printed in the United States of America

FOR LOUISE AND TWO SUSANS

# preface

This is not a history of modern American art. It is an attempt to define and trace the development of the chief movements in our painting and sculpture during the last fifty years, with occasional excursions into architecture and the graphic arts when these could help to clarify the central subject. It is little concerned with artistic personalities or with biographical information, but it does consider certain problems related to the position of the artist and his work in our present-day society.

The great diversity of our modern art is a measure, I believe, of its strength and vitality; but this has also contributed to the bewilderment of the intelligent public and has given, at times, a false impression of instability and confusion. I have tried, therefore, to make this a study of the underlying patterns of growth in our art, to show the broad paths along which it has moved and is now moving and to map the course of these as they cross and recross, join and separate, in an order that is complex but comprehensible.

In doing this, I have attempted to avoid a partisan position in regard to the relative merits of our various movements, for we are still too close to them to measure accurately their creative content. Recent reversals of critical judgments, such as that which reinstated the Hudson River School in favor, should be sufficient warning. I must admit that evaluations are inevitable at many points and are further implied by my omissions of most academic and commercial art, which seem obviously outside the creative field but conceivably may not be. Aside from these, however, I believe that there is still such genuine vitality in movements as far apart as abstraction and extreme realism that no fair picture of our art can afford to ignore either one or the other.

I am aware of the dangers which attend a search for general, rather than individual, forms of expression. I know the dismal view which artists and many others take of the "maniacs of classification" and their objection that this method forces square pegs into round holes and labels the artist according to his most prominent characteristic, whereas his work may in fact be much more varied. I have tried to avoid this pitfall by separating the different phases of such artists' work; a painter like Sheeler is discussed, for instance, both in the chapters on abstraction and on realism. This is admittedly a drawback to the interpretation of individual accomplishments, but that is not the purpose of this book, and it is only by such a method that one can classify without doing severe injustice to those varied talents who have worked in several directions.

And classification is surely necessary if we are to perceive the order underlying the great diversity of modern art. Yet here a further danger arises: that in defining this order we may oversimplify it and thereby seriously falsify the truth. I have tried to guard against this by keeping my categories as elastic as possible, by frequently indicating the points at which they blend into one another, and by admitting freely that much art lies in these overlapping zones and could be considered with some justice under more than one heading. It is only fair to add that movements do exist and have objective reality. They are not arbitrary devices of the critic, nor are they merely the sum of accidental similarities. The creative vision, in spite of a growing emphasis on individuality, is still widely shared. A movement is the result of this sharing, the result of common interests, aims, attitudes, and methods. Furthermore, the great majority of our art falls clearly enough within one or another and may justly be considered in relation to the larger trend to which it belongs.

What these movements are, their relation to each other, and their development in the last half century are briefly outlined in Chapter I. Thereafter I have considered first those movements which were revolutionary either in subject or in form, because these are plainly the most important. Not only do they account for a large part of our modern art, but they have also affected in one way or another the more conservative and traditional movements which have survived from the nineteenth century.

Many of these traditional forms have shown an amazing longevity. To a very small extent, this may be due to the fact that they have occasionally drawn a counterrevolutionary zeal from their crusade against modernism. To a much greater extent it is due to the fact that they have generally compromised with modernism, absorbing new life from the latter and gradually transforming themselves in the direction of the more advanced movements without losing their own distinctive qualities. In discussing these traditional movements, I have sketched in their nineteenth-century backgrounds, have shown in some detail their condition about 1900, and in tracing their subsequent growth or decay have tried to show the ways in which they were modified or refused to be modified by modernism.

I have devoted the last three chapters to the consideration of several problems which cut across movements and styles: the position of the artist in our modern civilization, certain present-day trends, both in art and in criticism, and the knotty question of what constitutes American art and in what ways it differs or fails to differ from that of Europe. Among the current trends, I have examined at some length the reactionary attacks of recent years on the more advanced movements and have tried to point out both the justice and the unfairness in the more thoughtful of these. Those who feel that the earlier chapters on expressionism, surrealism, and abstract art do not pay sufficient attention to the arguments which have repeatedly been raised against them may care to read in advance this part of Chapter XI.

This book could not have been written without the sympathetic assistance of many living artists and their dealers. I am afraid that some will find scant reward in the brevity with which I have been forced to consider them and in the generalized way in which their work has been treated. I can only reiterate that this is a study of the general rather than the particular and that I have had to seek basic similarities rather than personal variations. I am nonetheless grateful and hope that in the end this method may help in its way to spread a wider understanding of their aims.

I am inevitably indebted to the many devoted critics and historians of modern art whose courageous defense of the artist's right to seek truth in his own way has played so great a part in the long, uphill struggle of the modern movements. They are too numerous to be listed here, but I must acknowledge my special debt to Lloyd Goodrich, whose own writings and whose detailed criticism of this manuscript were of the greatest assistance. I have also leaned heavily, as anyone in this field must, on the critical and historical labors of Alfred H. Barr, Jr., James Thrall Soby, and Miss Dorothy Miller of the Museum of Modern Art. I am grateful to Holger Cahill for his freely given information on the little-known Inje-Inje movement of which he was the founder. The photographic records of the Whitney Museum of American Art and the American Art Research Council were immensely useful in studying the early work of several of our pioneer modernists; I am indebted to Miss Rosalind Irvine for her assistance in consulting these.

Finally I must record my debt to the Trustees of The Brooklyn Museum and to its Director, Charles Nagel, Jr., for their kindness in giving me leave of absence to write this book; also my great obligation to the Museum's Librarian, Mrs. Grace W. Banker, for her assistance in research.

J. I. H. B.
June 1950

# introduction to the paperback edition*

This book was written in 1949 and first published in 1951. This explains, I trust, why a number of important movements, from abstract expressionism to minimal art, are not covered in the original text. Because of the peculiar structure of the book (which is explained in the Preface), it did not seem feasible to attempt to bring it up to date, since this would have required rewriting nearly every chapter. The present introduction is offered as a second-best solution—a thumbnail sketch of the new developments that have occurred in the last eighteen years.

I do not know when the words "abstract expressionism" first became associated with a group of New York painters (Pollock, Kline, Hofmann, de Kooning, *et al.*) and the work that they did from the middle 1940's through the decade of the 1950's. In my original text I used the term to describe not only the beginnings of this movement, then scarcely defined, but also certain earlier free-form abstractions such as those done by Marsden Hartley and Max Weber near the beginning of the century. Common usage has established the more restricted meaning of the term, however, and I have conformed to this in the following pages.

There can be no doubt that abstract expressionism, or action painting, as it is sometimes called, was the dominant movement of the 1950's. To surrealism it owed two of its theoretical principles: automatism and a certain anti-aesthetic bias. Its spiritual ancestor was the early abstract work of Kandinsky; its immediate forerunners were Mark Tobey, who had developed a kind of semi-automatic "white writing" after a trip to China in 1934, and the fluid abstract imagery that Arshile Gorky created about 1940. It began to emerge as a recognizable movement in certain paintings by Hans Hofmann in 1943 and by Jackson Pollock in 1947. By the early 1950's it had become the

* Portions of this Introduction were originally written by John I. H. Baur for an article that appeared in the *Chicago Tribune Sunday Magazine Section*, April 23, 1967.

dominant mode of painting in the United States and its influence had begun to spread through virtually all the free world.

In essence, abstract expressionism is a theory, rather than a style. It is based on the premise that the action of the hand, uninfluenced by aesthetic considerations, can embody psychological impulses on the canvas. In practice, however, a more complex process is involved. Aesthetic preoccupations are actually seldom absent, and they are pitted against automatism and accident in a difficult, nearly unresolvable conflict, which is often further complicated by the demands of an obsessive imagery and the tensions between the nature of painting as a two-dimensional art and the persistent illusion of depth. A hard-won equilibrium between these warring elements is what the best of the abstract expressionists have achieved.

While the movement is not a homogeneous style, it has nevertheless developed a certain basic vocabulary, used separately or in combination by different artists. The calligraphy of Tobey and Pollock is one element—an expressive handwriting of brushed or dripped or spattered pigment remarkably evocative of personality and mood. In the hands of Franz Kline this became massive black hieroglyphs of tremendous weight and power, while in Philip Guston's early abstractions it was a maze of probing, questing lines almost painful in their intensity. Another element in the vocabulary is the individual brushstroke, of which Hofmann was a master—separate touches of paint which, by their weight, direction, texture, and relation to other strokes, imprint character on the canvas as surely as does calligraphy. A third element is the fluid, amorphous forms of Gorky, with their mysterious suggestions of organic life—associations that are even stronger in the work of William Baziotes and in some paintings of Theodoros Stamos. Still another element might be called the principle of envelopment as it was exercised in huge canvases by Mark Rothko and Barnett Newman, in which simple areas of vibrating color seem to engulf the spectator. The variations on this basic vocabulary have been nearly endless.

Two new movements have challenged the pre-eminence of abstract expressionism in the 1960's. The first of these is so-called hard-edge abstraction, a basically different kind of geometry from that of the past. There is, of course, nothing new about geometrical abstraction per se; Mondrian, Constructivism, the Bauhaus have all influenced American artists at one time or another. But the new movement has turned away from the classical tradition of clarity, intellectual control, and purely formal relationships, and has transformed geometry into a more romantic art. Josef Albers, who helped bring the Bauhaus disciplines to America in the 1930's, is a link between the older and the newer groups. The color dynamics of his "Homage to the Square" series, begun in the early 1950's, introduced optical effects of motion and vibration into otherwise static compositions of extreme simplicity, subtly disrupting their equilibrium. At about the same time Ad Reinhardt began a long sequence of geometrical paintings in which he drew ever darker veils across the color until now his rectangles have nearly disappeared in an enveloping blackness. In the work of other artists, such as Morris Louis, Kenneth Noland, and Richard Anuszkiewicz, the exploration of optics and color-motion has been pushed to extremes, while their generally simple, symmetrical designs have often been blurred along the edges (despite the hard-edge label) so that the geometry seems in imminent danger of dissolving. A feeling of mystery, of a pulsating inner life, informs their work. It is this that makes hard-edge abstraction so different from the geometry of the past.

But the most direct challenge to abstract expressionism in recent times is that spontaneous eruption of the 1960's known as Pop Art, or the New Realism. A movement of deliberate vulgarity, it takes both its subjects and its styles from the commercial commonplaces of our day—from billboards, comic strips, newsreel movies, advertisements, supermarket displays, and the like. Its concern with such unfashionable urban material makes it the spiritual descendant of the Ash Can School founded by the Eight a half-century earlier. The Pop artists are more truly revolutionary, for they have identified themselves with this tawdry world rather than commenting on it from without. Insofar as possible, they have suppressed the marks of individual style and have imitated, often with *trompe l'oeil* accuracy, the anonymous techniques and conventions of commercial art. The only obvious liberty that they have sometimes allowed themselves has been a vast enlargement of their subjects—a process that has contradictory effects in that it emphasizes the coarseness and vulgarity of the original image yet at the same time gives it an almost abstract configuration. Jasper Johns and Robert Rauschenberg were pioneers in the movement, but both have moved away from its main course. It was developed principally by Jim Dine, Marisol, Claes Oldenburg, James Rosenquist, Andy Warhol, and several dozen equally gifted artists.

Today Pop and Op appear to be blending and moving toward other concepts. They always had in common an impersonality and a largeness of scale. These are the characteristics of the so-called minimal, or ABC art, such as the structures of Robert Morris and ~~David~~ Donald Judd, which are less sculpture than a three-dimensional equivalent of hard-edge abstraction. As scale has grown and art has expanded from the flat plane, it has begun to surround and engulf the spectator, becoming a complete environment rather than an object. Within this environment optical sensations have been heightened by the use of neon tubing in brilliant colors and a variety of flashing, projected or diffracted lights, as in the elaborate structures of USCO, a group of multimedia artists. Sound, smell, and tactile sensations have been added. Sometimes the effect is predominantly abstract, sometimes Pop references persist, almost casually, while in the work of Edward Kienholz the Pop element has been transformed from something cool and detached to a passionate involvement with social issues.

These seem to me the most lively innovations in American art since this book was written. But I do not mean to imply that they constitute the only creative work of the last eighteen years. Our realists, our precisionists, our expressionists and romantic visionaries, our painters of social comment, our older geometrical abstractionists, and even some of our surrealists have continued through part or all of this period to do work of force and distinction. But the directions they have followed have not differed greatly, in most cases, from those established by their earlier work. These directions are the ones that I tried to anatomize when I first set out to write this book, and while I would change many things if I could do it over today—especially in matters of example and emphasis—I believe that the main pattern is still a reasonably accurate portrayal of the state of American art at mid-century and of how it got that way. More of that pattern persists now, some two decades later, than we sometimes realize, for many older currents in American art continue to flow strongly beneath the agitated surface of the present.

JOHN I. H. BAUR

*May 1967*

# contents

# list of illustrations

(illustrations follow page 154)

**xix**

**xxi**

xxii

REVOLUTION AND TRADITION IN

# modern american art

# 1

## A SURVEY

During the past fifty years, American art has undergone a more profound transformation than at any time in our history. This is also true
of European art, but in this country the changes were more radical
because we were less adequately prepared for them. Throughout the
nineteenth century we had lagged nearly a generation behind the new
movements abroad, such as the innovations of the Barbizon School and
the French impressionists. We had, to be sure, developed several characteristic movements of our own which owed relatively little to
European sources, but these were the flowering of a long realist tradition in American art and their very persistence made it more difficult
for us to accept the revolutionary forms of modernism.

Theoretically, this might have been an advantage if we could have
preserved the creative vigor of our native movements and ignored the
new "isms" of Europe, although such a course was never a real possibility. By the year 1900 the sinews of American art had weakened
badly. Two of our greatest painters, Winslow Homer and Thomas
Eakins, were still active, but both had already said what appeared to be
the last word in movements born some half a century earlier. Each
was a culmination — Eakins of a bare and penetrating realism, Homer
of a vigorous impressionism modified by the same realism. Albert P.
Ryder was a figure apart, a recluse and a visionary, whose more truly
revolutionary work would not be appreciated until after the disruption
of realism's long dominion.

If we look elsewhere, the signs of a perilous anemia are apparent
enough. By 1900 the influence of Whistler and the Barbizon School,

3

which had united in a group sometimes called the Tonalists, had worn to a transparent thinness. The American impressionists, never very robust, had already done their best work. A large group of decorative painters under the influence of John La Farge and Kenyon Cox were exploring a sterile vein of sentiment in the neoclassical and neorenaissance manner. The slashing brushwork of Sargent, Duveneck, and Chase was still lively but already it was being transformed into an academic formula. The Society of American Artists, which had once revolted against the conservatism of the National Academy, was now so staid that it would soon merge with the older body.

Perhaps at no time has our art been more truly provincial or more intolerant of any stylistic deviations. When, for instance, the decorative *art nouveau* style reached America early in the present century, it was looked upon as "revolutionary and therefore to be doubted . . . most dangerous and threatening." The distortions of caricature encountered, said Benjamin De Casseres, "the Anglo-Saxon injunction: Thou shalt not commit irony!" Even our own colonial portraits were considered by some "ligneous, marmoreal and air-tight as a carriage painter's decorations," while Gilbert Stuart was preferred to John Singleton Copley because the latter "painted the pride and vanity of life. Stuart went to the real man." [1]

This condition lasted virtually unchallenged until about 1908, but in that year two portentous events occurred. A group of New York artists who called themselves the Eight * held an exhibition at the Macbeth Gallery, and a dealer named Alfred Stieglitz showed the work of the French modernist, Henri Matisse. The Eight were far from homogeneous and soon disbanded without exhibiting again, but their name has been firmly attached, both then and since, to the exploration of a radically new subject matter which gave for a time a new lease on life to the traditional styles in which they worked. The Matisse show was small and included no large or important pictures, but it was the first to introduce any aspect of French modernism to America and it inaugurated Stieglitz's long campaign to win acceptance here for the

* Arthur B. Davies, William Glackens, Robert Henri, Ernest Lawson, George Luks, Maurice Prendergast, Everett Shinn, and John Sloan.

pioneers of abstract and expressionist art, both foreign and native. For the first time in many years American art found that it had not one but two revolutions on its hands, and these were opposed in character.

The Eight, in searching out the unconventional aspects of urban life, asserted a social liberalism as radical in its day as their styles were conservative. Our early modernists, on the other hand, were generally conventional in their choice of subject but in style they flouted the long realist tradition in American art and fashioned a profounder revolution, which has not yet run its course. They too were far from homogeneous. In one group were the expressionists who distorted the visual world for a heightened emotional effect; in the other were the abstractionists who turned the world into formal patterns in which recognizable objects nearly or entirely disappeared. In spite of much mingling, the two movements have followed rather different courses in this country. Expressionism has grown slowly and steadily during the last forty years while abstract art has developed in three more or less distinct waves, each more widespread than the preceding.

From 1908 to 1913 the social revolution of the Eight was dominant, both because it was better known and because it was more easily understood, even by those who deplored it. During the same years the formal revolution of the modernists was scarcely known outside the small circle which frequented Stieglitz's gallery, and to most American critics it was blankly incomprehensible. The balance was changed, however, by the now famous Armory Show of 1913, which has been so often and so fully described that we need only recall its salient points.

Organized by a group of artists who called themselves the Association of American Painters and Sculptors, the exhibition, as it finally took form in the Sixty-ninth Regiment Armory on Lexington Avenue, was a huge and sprawling affair in which some sixteen hundred works were shown. Most of the pioneer American modernists were included but their work was almost lost in a flood of more conservative paintings, for the American section comprised roughly three quarters of the whole. Modern German, Italian, and English painting was represented scantly or not at all. But the large French section, which accounted for the remainder of the exhibition, introduced to America a striking selection of the principal modernists, both cubist and Fauve, as well as the work of their predecessors, Cézanne, Gauguin, and Van Gogh.

In a statement to the public Arthur B. Davies, president of the association, announced that "the Society has embarked on no propaganda. It proposes to enter on no controversy," its object being only to present modern art "so that the intelligent may judge for themselves." But inevitably the exhibition was taken as a militant gesture in defense of modernism, an impression heightened by Frederick James Gregg's foreword to the catalogue in which he suggested that American artists might well consider "whether or not [they] . . . have fallen behind," and concluding: "Art is a sign of life. There can be no life without change. . . . To be afraid of what is different or unfamiliar, is to be afraid of life. . . . This exhibition is an indication that the Association of American Painters and Sculptors is against cowardice even when it takes the form of amiable self-satisfaction." [2]

This did nothing to soften the reaction of the public and of most critics, who agreed with Royal Cortissoz in calling all French painting from Cézanne on "a gospel of studied license and self assertion," fit only for "the rubbish heap." The condemnation was strong, but perhaps no stronger than that which had met the French moderns in Paris a few years earlier. Here, too, more understanding voices were raised at once in their support. W. D. MacColl spoke out for Matisse, and Guy du Bois tried to make Americans understand the significance of Cézanne and of the cubists, who "have realized most the importance of this classical order." [3]

The effects of the controversy were healthy, for it stimulated an interest in art and the modern movements which was unprecedented in America. "It is probably safe to say," reported one magazine, "that no phase of political life or professional activity, no condition of progress in the country has been so widely and incessantly discussed this season as *art*, new and old." The exhibition went on, in abbreviated form, from New York to Chicago, then to Boston. It was seen, Lloyd Goodrich estimates, by perhaps a quarter of a million people in all. [4]

While the Eight and their circle were partially eclipsed by the

6

Armory Show and by the wave of abstract and expressionist art which followed it, another group of more conservative artists, whom we have called the romantic realists, found that certain elements of the modern movements could be grafted to the Homer-Eakins tradition by means of a simplification of form and the suppression of detail. At the beginning — that is, about 1910–1920 — this was a not entirely successful compromise, for it lacked both the warm humanity of the Eight and the formal boldness of the more advanced artists. After 1920, however, the movement was greatly enriched by the addition of many of our pioneer modernists who abandoned their experiments with abstraction and expressionism to return to a realism modified by a deeper understanding of the principles behind the modern movements.

The year 1920 may be taken, indeed, as the dividing line between our first and second waves of abstract art and as a moment of limited reaction against modernism in general. This reaction was not solely in a conservative direction. The Dada movement, which turned abstraction into an art of mockery and the irrational, was a reflection of postwar disillusion, but it also aimed at the destruction of cubism's intellectual basis. Dada was largely a European movement, in the years 1916–1922, but it had, as we shall see, both repercussions and parallels in America.

Of much greater importance was the fruitful and creative compromise between abstraction and realism which was wrought during the 1920's by the group sometimes known as the Immaculates. In a way this compromise was similar to the one which the romantic realists had fashioned earlier in that it was based on a simplification of forms and the suppression of detail. But it was much more strongly abstract in character and its simplifications were applied with better logic to the machine and engineering forms of our industrial civilization rather than to the Homeric landscape and the Eakins figure. Its immaculately patterned pictures became, therefore, a comprehensible expression of American life and the first important bridge between native tradition and the modern vision.

The Immaculates were the backbone of our second period of abstract art in the 1920's, but they were joined in the same decade by a

**7**

considerable number of futurists, who sought to infuse the generally static patterns of abstract art with dynamic motion. Both groups were concerned with the machine as a symbol of twentieth-century America but the futurists, with a few exceptions, caught only its most romantic and superficial aspects while the Immaculates penetrated more deeply the lessons of function and order which it imposed.

The economic depression of the 1930's virtually ended the second wave of abstract art in this country. The suffering of those years turned increasing numbers of artists to the consideration of man as a social being and to specific problems of social relations which were not susceptible to abstract treatment. Nevertheless, much of the realist art which inevitably followed was colored by the Immaculate vision, while expressionism, the other great branch of the modern movement, adapted itself readily to the new conditions. Expressionism became, indeed, the chief weapon of a group of painters who were primarily concerned with the class struggle between labor and capital and who used its formal distortions to attack privilege and expose with new vigor the miseries of poverty and unemployment.

Not all American art of the 1930's was socially conscious, but very nearly all reflected the trend towards increased realism which came in the wake of the depression. The romantic realist movement reached its peak in this decade, partly because it broke the bounds of its earlier, conventional subject matter and explored new aspects of the American scene somewhat as the Eight had done, though more inclusively. The poetry of the city and its poor were rediscovered by a group which centered in New York's Fourteenth Street. In the middle west a militant regionalism sprang up under the banner of the American Scene. Both of these movements drew a wide following although many of the best romantic realists of the period remained outside their borders.

A more uncompromising realism — spare, penetrating, and unromanticized or at least less obviously romanticized — was also reborn at about this time. It served no special group or interests and is found as often among the painters of social comment as among those devoted to the conventional subjects of landscape, figure, and still life. In part it was a revival of a strong native tradition, in part it was inspired by the newly imported surrealism, which colored some of its manifestations.

Abroad, surrealism had sprung from the dying Dada movement about 1924, but it did not reach America until the early 1930's. In spite of the interest which it aroused, pure surrealism, with its insistence on automatism and the searching of the subconscious mind, had few direct followers here. Nevertheless, its influence was pervasive and has grown steadily in the last two decades. This influence has been greatest, perhaps, on the younger abstract painters of the 1940's.

As early as 1935 abstract art began again, for the third time, to capture the creative imagination of the American artist. At first the movement developed slowly, but after 1940 it became, for the first time in our history, the dominant one in American art. This was partly due to the fresh channels which surrealism opened into romantic territory. But our modern abstract art has also reëxplored its earlier European sources and its earlier native traditions and has devised many new forms through the crossing of these with each other and with surrealism.

Expressionism also has flourished in the last ten years. If it has made fewer new discoveries, this may be due to the movement's more consistent development from the early years of the century, which has already established a firmer and less volatile tradition than that which has governed our abstract work. Today expressionism, in its representational forms, no longer seems so radical a departure from our art of the past.

Realism has somewhat waned in the decade of the 1940's. This is particularly true of romantic realism and of that American-scene regionalism which formed a part of the movement. Regionalism has succumbed, though never entirely, to a spirit of internationalism closely associated with the second World War. But quite aside from this, romantic realism, as a style, has shown signs of diminishing creative vigor for complex reasons which we will discuss later. Extreme realism, on the other hand, has lost little ground and has even perhaps gained in recent years.

Finally, two traditional kinds of painters — our primitives (that is, our untrained or unsophisticated artists) and those poets of the inner eye whom we have called romantic visionaries — have persisted throughout the last half century with little regard to the fluctuations of the more sophisticated movements. In some instances, however, the experiments of the modernists have had at least an oblique influence on the painters of the second group and perhaps even on those of the first. It is also apparent that the growing acceptance of abstract art has widened the general appreciation of our primitives, both past and present, while surrealism has paved the way for a new evaluation of our romantic visionaries. In spite of these relations, our primitive art and our visionary art are essentially traditional since both kinds flourished for at least a hundred years before the present century. This does not mean that a continuous line of development can be traced in either, but rather that each has occurred spontaneously and sporadically through a long period in our history.

In the most general terms, this is the pattern of American art as it has been woven during the last fifty years. Reversing that historical process, we shall try to unravel the threads of the major movements and examine each separately.

# 2

REVOLUTION IN SUBJECT

## the american scene

At no time in our history has subject matter been of minor concern to most American artists. The discovery of native landscape and genre in the nineteenth century, like the discovery of industrial America in the twentieth, released new waves of feeling and new formal experiments in which to embody them. Not all innovations in form have grown, of course, from the exploration of new subjects nor have the latter always produced formal consequences of importance. But it has often been true that great changes in our art seem to be linked with the examination of new aspects of life or nature. The shifting field of the creative vision in the last half century tells us much, therefore, of the history of our modern art, though it is only one part of a complex development.

If new subjects have been the cause of revolution, old ones have also served the forces of reaction. Stereotyped themes, long repeated, have often preserved, by their unconscious dominion over the mind, outworn styles which might otherwise have perished sooner. In 1900 American art suffered this condition perhaps more unrelievedly than at any time in our history. The convention in landscape had long ago swung from the panoramic view to the intimate "bit," the small motif of garden, fence corner, swamp, or meadow. "Distance," remarked a critic in 1893, "was wiped out by a high sky line or smothered in fog or mist, and mountains were voted *banal*." [1] In figure painting the maiden in neoclassical drapery was ubiquitous; she was posed by Carrol Beckwith in a treetop as "Spring" or by Will H. Low on a haystack as "Autumn." Genre painting had descended to an incredible senti-

11

mentality. Every Academy annual was sprinkled with pictures called "Dream Life," "Divinity of Motherhood," "Love's Token," "Day Dreams," "Entourée des Roses," and the like. Subjects of this kind had, through long repetition, established their exclusive right to the artist's attention. They were the intrinsically "beautiful" themes which Bliss Carman had in mind when he wrote that "the business of art is to afford joyance"; it then followed that "since few can live as joyously as they would, what a shame it is that great gifts of expression should ever be wasted on heinous and joyless subjects." [2]

The importance of subject had, of course, a legitimate place in the realist philosophy which dominated American art throughout the nineteenth century. In its purest form this philosophy held that the task of the artist is to reveal an objective and preëxisting beauty in nature rather than create a new beauty in terms of art. "Nature paints the best part of the picture"; the painter then must be supremely sensitive to those most lovely and moving aspects of the visual world so that he may discover and mirror them for the delight of less perceptive eyes. This thought, which lay at the center of so much nineteenth-century aesthetic belief, persisted long and vigorously in the twentieth. "The best rule of all," Birge Harrison told his pupils at the Art Students League in 1910, "is to keep the eyes always wide open and observant of the things about you, for the most beautiful compositions in the world are always the daring and unexpected arrangements of nature. It behooves us to see them." And the conclusion which Harrison, like many others, drew was that "Nature is not all beautiful by any means. But why should we choose to perpetuate her ugly side? I believe it to be one of the artist's chief functions, as it should be his chief delight, to watch for the rare mood when she wafts aside the veil of the commonplace and shows us her inner soul in some bewildering vision of poetic beauty." How little change there had been in the half century since Asher B. Durand had advised an imaginary pupil: "Nature herself is unequal, in the eye of Art. It is the province of Art, then, and all the licence that the artist can claim or desire is to choose the time and place where she displays her chief perfections." [3]

It was perhaps inevitable that the philosophy which produced much

**12**

creative work in the 1850's was no longer capable, without modification, of serving the twentieth-century artist as well. The vision of nature's perfections, which to Durand had had the force of religious revelation, the rural episodes which Mount had translated into visual folk poetry, even the limited excitement with which La Farge had rediscovered Greek and Renaissance art — these had lost by 1900 their freshness and their power to evoke wonder, except in the hands of individuals like Homer and Eakins, whose art belonged essentially to the preceding century.

Of the formal revolution which finally disrupted and denied every aspect of realist philosophy we shall write later. It was narrowly preceded by a revolution in subject matter which breathed new life into the old beliefs, a revolution which has flared twice in the last fifty years, first in opposition to academic art, later in partial opposition to "modern," especially abstract, art. This we shall consider now solely in respect to subject matter, for in practice it clothed itself in several quite different styles which can be discussed more logically elsewhere.

The first phase of the revolution opened to the artist the rich vein of humanity in urban and industrial America — the teeming life of slums, markets, saloons, factories, workshops, cheap theaters, and poolrooms. It created a new kind of genre painting with a new set of characters — peddlers, prostitutes, pugilists, orators, and the vivid types of Irish, Italian, and Jewish immigrants. This was a phase of American life with more than its share of poverty and suffering but rich, too, in color, in humor and vitality. Mushrooming into existence after the Civil War, it had been almost totally neglected, for obvious reasons, by the American artist.

Almost, but not quite. Isolated here and there through the last thirty years of the nineteenth century one finds the stirrings of a new interest. "There be more joy," wrote W. Mackay Laffan in 1880, "over one honest and sincere American horse pond, over one truthful and dirty tenement, over one unaffected sugar refinery, over one vulgar but unostentatious coal wharf than there shall be over ninety and nine

**13**

mosques of St. Sophia, Golden Horns, Normandy Cathedrals, and all the rest of the holy conventionalities and orthodox bosh." [4]

In the same decade, Charles W. Larned pleaded a like cause. "Humanity is no less human now than in the past, and in man's humanity lie the noblest subjects of art. . . . We are sick of Greek myths, we are weary of artificialities. Go out into the highways of life, artists of today, and paint us the tragedies, the comedies, beauties, hopes, aspirations and fears that live; 'bring in the poor, and the maimed, and the halt, and the blind,' with the rest, and let us see the panorama of life more before us. Go out and see them for yourselves, feel them, understand them, love them — you cannot 'chic them up' in your studios. You must be keen observers, close students of men and nature — not for their 'tonality,' their 'values,' and their 'composition' alone, but for their loves and their hates, their beliefs and their doubts, their joys and their sorrows, their beauty and ugliness." [5]

Even earlier, artists had begun to pioneer in this direction. John F. Weir, son of an instructor in art at West Point, had painted in 1867 "The Gun Foundry" and the following year "Forging the Shaft," perhaps our first pictures of the modern industrial scene. In New York a few years later Louis C. Tiffany enlarged his interest in rural genre to portray the dilapidated shops and tenements of the city with a new feeling for their human warmth and picturesqueness. His painting "Old New York," with Ralph A. Blakelock's somewhat similar scenes of the shanties which rimmed the city, marks the beginning of a new approach to the urban landscape. All of the above were painted probably in the late sixties or seventies. During the next two decades others, like Jerome Myers, Charles F. Ulrich, and August Franzen, discovered similar themes. Myers, especially, was moved by the rich humanity of New York's lower East Side, which he began to paint about 1887. "Others saw ugliness and degradation there," he wrote later. "I saw poetry and beauty. I took a sporting chance of saying something out of my own experience and risking whether it was worthwhile or not. That is all any artist can do." [6]

And the truth is that, before Myers, none of the artists who had essayed these subjects had found them permanently "worthwhile"; at

14

least, none had pursued them for more than a few years. No movement had been founded, no public response awakened. The field, in 1900, was still virtually unplowed.

The revolution which finally changed all this is inextricably associated with the group of New York artists who called themselves the Eight, although actually only half its members were much involved in the new movement while many outside contributed heavily. But it was indeed the concerted action of the Eight in organizing, in proclaiming their revolt against the National Academy, and in holding their much publicized exhibition at the Macbeth Gallery in 1908 which first made the public aware that a new force had been liberated in American art. To the conservatives they were "The Revolutionary Gang," "The Black School," "The Ash Can School." But to many critics, like Giles Edgerton, who were still looking anxiously for signs of life in American art, still begging the artist to take advantage of "our towering, crude, vibrating, nervous, uncertain civilization," and to give us pictures of "our East Side polyglot populace," the Eight were "creating a national art," and their exhibition was "undoubtedly the greatest event of the season in the American art world." [7]

The four members of the group at the center of the controversy were John Sloan, George Luks, William Glackens, and Everett Shinn. All were able illustrators whose pictorial reporting for various newspapers and magazines had opened their eyes to the wealth of pathetic, colorful, and heroic subjects in the urban scene. These they had begun to paint, a few years before their exhibition, with an enthusiasm and a sense of pioneering which had its literary parallel in the writings of Jack London and Frank Norris, with whom indeed they were occasionally compared.

Several other artists found their way to the same subject at almost the same time as the Eight. Eugene Higgins, returning from Paris in 1904, had already painted the poor, with a feeling, however, for the suffering and misery of their lot which was quite different from the vigorous optimism of the Eight. In like manner, the Swedish sculptor Charles Haag, who settled in America in 1903, found in his own youth of desperate poverty the motivation for several small bronzes caricatur-

**15**

ing the wealthy and exalting, perhaps for the first time in this country, the strike as a weapon in the class struggle. Both he and Higgins had an able apologist in the socialist, John Spargo, whose articles in *The Craftsman* pointed the economic moral of their work.

But for the most part the character of the new movement was stamped less by social consciousness than by the raffish gusto of Luks and Shinn, the shrewd and humane commentaries of Sloan, the gentle poetry of Myers, the humor and sensuous delight of Glackens. Its pioneers were extroverts who found, according to their different temperaments, an endless variety of rewarding experience and small cause for bitterness or disillusion in the multifaceted city.

In this case the city was almost exclusively New York, and the center of the new ferment lay close to the classroom of another member of the Eight, Robert Henri, who was perhaps the most liberal and influential teacher of his time. It was young "Henri men" who predominated in another revolutionary and specifically anti-Academy gesture in the same year as the Eight's exhibition, though less publicized and now largely forgotten. This was the first so-called Independent Show, organized on the spur of the moment by Arnold Friedman, Glenn Coleman, and Julius Golz, Jr., in the deserted quarters of the Harmonie Club on Forty-second Street facing Bryant Park. The lease, as Friedman wrote, grew in the eyes of the founding trio "till it assumed the proportions of a warrant, a death warrant to the Academy, no less." The exhibition could hardly live up to such expectations, however. "The reviewers treated it merely as another point to cover and the show without flourish passed into limbo." Nevertheless it had its critical admirers who found in it much "strong work that smacked decidedly of the ideas and ideals of 'the Eight,'" and who praised it for being "full of the New York of today," [8] and it gave encouragement to several young painters who were soon to make notable contributions to the new movement. Glenn Coleman's drawings of street scenes introduced, for example, a subtler sense of psychological drama and conflicts than had yet been attempted, while George Bellows rapidly outdid Luks in the muscular vigor of his dramatic prize-fight canvases.

In addition to Haag, a number of sculptors were also active in ex-

16

ploring the new subjects. Mahonri Young was modeling laborers and stevedores as early as 1904 and somewhat later he, too, turned to prize-fight subjects. In 1914, apparently influenced by Jane Addams' writings, the sculptress Abastenia St. Leger Eberle took a studio on Madison Street in New York's lower East Side where she turned out closely observed genre pieces such as "The Ragpicker" and "Roller Skating." In Chicago a group of young sculptors, many pupils of Lorado Taft, felt the same influences — among them, Gutzon Borglum, Charles J. Mulligan, and Laura Katz.

While little of the work produced was aimed specifically at social reform, almost all of it was marked by a broad humanitarianism which had a noteworthy effect at this time in the field of architecture. More than aesthetic considerations, it kept alive during a peculiarly barren period the ideal of functionalism, in the sense of building for human needs and comfort.

At various times in the nineteenth century this ideal had struggled to the surface, both in the theory of Horatio Greenough and others and in the practice of Henry Hobson Richardson and Louis H. Sullivan. But by 1900 it had been very nearly swamped in a wave of academic revivalism crested with McKim, Mead, and White's classical and renaissance forms. The practical opposition in the early 1900's was led by Sullivan's most brilliant disciple, Frank Lloyd Wright, whose formal accomplishments were more revolutionary than those of any American painter or sculptor of the time. But there was also a vigorous theoretical opposition which concerns us more here because it argued from a social rather than an aesthetic premise.

This was led, with bitter eloquence, by Sullivan himself, who saw in the pretentious buildings of the revivalists a symbol that "our civilization is not democratic as we fondly suppose, but utterly feudal through and through." Functionalism, to Sullivan, was efficiency, but not of a mechanical sort. "If it be asked, efficiency in what? the answer," he felt, "is clear; efficiency in social expression: that is to say in the expression of our real lives, our real beliefs, aspirations and hopes as a people." The argument was echoed by others. "We think to let the mantle of our education cover the bareness of popular apathy and

**17**

creative thought," wrote William L. Price. "We think to lift the masses
to an understanding of the excellency of revived styles and resurrected
cultures while we should be studying those very masses for an inspiration." [9]

Thus the socially conscious theories, which often found themselves
in opposition to modern aesthetic experiments, were not always so but
sometimes paralleled and reinforced them. This was not true of architecture alone. To the conservative public one of the most difficult
phases of modern painting was that which returned to the expressive
distortions of primitive art, such as African sculpture, for its inspiration.
Yet the social approach which would "study the masses" led logically,
as Price demonstrated, to the same simplest artistic denominator. The
"naked savage" as an artist "looks with new eyes on creation. . . And
the tale of that emotion is written large on pot and bow." So one
reaches by the social path the even more extreme conclusion that "this
is art, fine art, all there is to art, and it is enough." [10]

The revolution of the Eight did not, however, pursue social philosophy to such ends, nor did it for long keep its revolutionary character.
After its exhibition of 1908 the group dissolved as an organization,
realizing none of its announced program for annual shows to which
liberal foreign artists were to have been invited. Critics and public soon
accepted the new range of subjects while certain artists, especially
Bellows, enjoyed widespread popularity. There was indeed something
pathetic in the efforts of Luks to maintain his revolutionary status by
a determined bohemianism long after his art had become an accepted
convention.

The event which, more than anything else, obscured the revolutionary aspect of the Eight's work was the famous Armory Show of
1913 which for the first time made America uncomfortably aware of
the formal experiments of the French Fauves and cubists and of a few
American pioneers in the same vein. The abstract art which spread
rapidly to so many younger painters in the wake of this event seemed,
and indeed was, incomparably more radical than social realism.

The story of this formal revolution will be told elsewhere; here we need note only that its first wave, which occurred roughly at the time of the Armory Show, and a lesser second wave, which followed closely about 1920, engulfed and dissipated for over a decade the forces which the Eight had liberated. But these were dormant rather than vanquished. When they began to revive in the middle twenties and especially during their culmination in the thirties, they showed an extraordinary vitality which in turn threatened to rout the cause of abstraction in America.

During these later years the new movement widened its scope to reëxamine rural and small-town America as well as her urban and industrial life, sharpened its comments on social injustice, and explored with greater diligence many more phases of our civilization. Its leaders were men of genuine creative power who differed widely both in their styles and in their approach to the American scene. Closest to the Eight in spirit was a group which might be called the Fourteenth Street school, for their studios were clustered in New York's Greenwich Village and their subjects were drawn largely from the street life of that region and its summer resort, Coney Island. Many were students of Kenneth Hayes Miller, who was himself of the generation of the Eight although he did not start painting his characteristic shoppers and street crowds until the mid 1920's or slightly later. At the center of the group were — and still are — the three Soyer brothers, Raphael, Moses, and Isaac. Going beyond Miller and the Eight, they explored every aspect of life among the city's poor with a tenderness, a warmth of sentiment and genuine understanding of their subject which was deeper than Miller's cool detachment and avoided the picturesqueness which had colored Luks's or Shinn's treatment of similar themes. Of the older men, they were closest perhaps to Sloan, although a gentle melancholy which runs through their work is quite different from his buoyant optimism. The school has also spread in many other directions. Reginald Marsh added to the iconography of the city the desolate flophouses of the Bowery, the raffish glitter of the burlesque show, and the sensually mingled bodies on the beach at Coney. Chaim Gross preserved the involutions of the circus acrobats in stone and wood. Outside New York other painters, like Aaron Bohrod in Chicago, followed similar paths.

After 1930 the bread line, the employment office, the life on park benches, and all the other pitiful appurtenances of the depression were faithfully recorded by this group with a somber realization of what these meant in terms of human suffering. Yet the mood in which they painted them was often closer to resignation than it was to protest. It remained for a different group of socially conscious painters to wage a sharp battle against the conditions of those years. One of the first was William Gropper, who was soon joined by Ben Shahn, Philip Evergood, Jack Levine, Robert Gwathmey, and others. These men found in poverty no redeeming poetry but only a condition which debased humanity. Their poor were revealed with a bitter force which made those of the Eight seem, by comparison, romantic fictions. On the rich and the privileged, the lawmakers and the law enforcers, they poured a concentrated vitriol. They were idealists and reformers who brought to American art a crusading zeal and a rebellious spirit which it had seldom seen before. In their use of the brush as a social weapon they enlarged the concept of art's function as radically in their own way as the abstract artists had done on a chiefly aesthetic level.

Outside of these loosely knit groups many individual painters discovered new and unexploited aspects of contemporary life. Fletcher Martin captured the excitement of baseball. Joseph Hirsch caught the gestures and self-importance of the American business man. Edward Hopper revealed the loneliness of city rooms, of hotel lobbies and movie palaces; Charles Burchfield, the haunted forms of Victorian architecture and the drabness of suburban streets. Even sculpture broke with its conventions and experimented with genre scenes which involved complex groupings and pictorial settings. Mahonri Young had pioneered in this direction early in the century; during the 1930's he was joined by many younger men such as Harry Wickey, Chaim Gross, Robert Cronbach, and John Hovannes.

All of the many genuinely creative artists in these various groups did more than hold a mirror to our sprawling culture; they selected, intensified, and wrought a new iconography of American life. As their images became impressed on our consciousness during the decade of the 1930's, however, a legion of less talented artists worked them over in endless variations until they were nearly wrung dry of meaning. The Coney Island beach, the burlesque show, the shanty town behind the factory became themes into which it was increasingly difficult to breathe new life. Inevitably, perhaps, they began to assume a mystical significance of their own, not because they were capable of releasing that emotion necessary to genuine creation, but solely because they were distinctively American and the established symbols of a national art. Thus there grew in some quarters an artistic chauvinism which held that "the very nationalistic spirit which is in many things narrowing . . . seems to foster in the arts a necessary and beautiful strength," [11] but which in fact led to a kind of pictorial inbreeding.

This tendency was strengthened by the fact that the American Scene movement was in part a revolt against international modernism. At the beginning there was perhaps some justification for the prevalent feeling that American painters and sculptors had swallowed an indigestible lump of modern French aesthetics. This was only true of our minor artists, but these had multiplied so rapidly by the early 1920's that even intelligent critics who had been friendly to the modern cause became alarmed. "The bandwagon of 'modernism,' " said Forbes Watson, "after a period of immense usefulness, is pretty well deserted and the word 'modern,' after fifteen years of perpetual strain, is an invalid requiring long rest and seclusion," a sentiment echoed by Virgil Barker when he wrote that the term "modernist" was "fast declining into semi-respectability; once the rallying-cry of a hard and honorable fight, it is being progressively debased through its appropriation by every month's freak gallery-exhibitionist." There were, of course, even less sympathetic voices. Leo Stein had come to feel that "Picasso has been typically disastrous in his influence," while many conservatives, like Oliver Tonks, accused abstract art of its failure to communicate: "One may even go so far as to agree that, even if the idea is not comprehensible now, it may be some day. . . But at present, except to its creator, the work is without value." [12]

In the 1930's this attitude, greatly exaggerated, was taken over by a group which promoted an aggressive regionalism centering in the middle west and denying even to the eastern cities any part in its militant Americanism. To Thomas Craven, its principal spokesman, our eastern painters as a whole were "grovelling in the emasculated tradition of the French modernists," their pictures "a form of compensation common to failures and social outcasts, a psychological activity identical in more exalted spheres with the affectations of the classical counterparts of the artist — the whore and the bum." In their place he elevated the now famous "Triumvirate" as "the leaders of a new movement which has swept the country" and ended "American subservience to foreign cultural fashions." They were Thomas H. Benton, "most prominent, vigorous, versatile of our painters," John Steuart Curry, whose best work "makes most Cézannes look faint, painfully hacked together and emotionally empty," and Grant Wood, "the designer of regional forms which have no parallel in modern art." [13]

The critical excesses of Craven, which were occasionally echoed by Benton and Wood, have obscured to some degree the real contributions which the members of the triumvirate made. All of them found in regionalism, at least for a time, a genuine faith and a deeply felt emotion which expressed itself in some memorable images of American life. If they could have escaped the extreme artistic isolationism which seems now, in retrospect, an unnecessary if understandable part of their philosophy, they might have prolonged the freshness of discovery and escaped the limiting dogma of a regionalism proclaimed for its own sake.

There are still many and excellent painters of the American scene — as there have been since the beginning of our art and doubtless will continue to be. In the larger sense all painting produced in the American environment belongs in this category, a simple truth which the extreme regionalists overlooked. The specific movement associated with the term, however, dwindled in the 1940's to a shadow of its earlier self. The factors which have determined its life span are too complex to be measured with finality, but a major one is doubtless that general reaction against isolationism and narrow nationalism that followed the second World War. Closely related is the growing interest of American artists in the more international style of abstract art which, for the third time in this century and more vigorously than ever before, has taken root on our soil.

# 3

## REVOLUTION IN SUBJECT

### the machine and the subconscious

Two other revolutions in subject matter have had important consequences for American art in this century. These, too, were clothed in a wide variety of styles ranging from abstraction to extreme realism. Like the movements inspired by the American scene, they owe their principal identity to their content rather than their form.

The first of these revolutions might better be called a skirmish in new territory. It was the discovery by the artist of the beauty in the machine and in those related functional forms of our industrial civilization such as the bridge and the grain elevator, a beauty of polished and smoothly working parts which came to symbolize for a number of our painters and sculptors and for even more of our architects the distinctive quality of our modern age.

The perception of this kind of beauty was not entirely a twentieth-century discovery. In 1856 Samuel Atkins Eliot had written: "Mathematics and machinery are not usually enumerated among the fine arts, properly so called, but . . . the lines and figures drawn by the scientific engineer often show the very curves which the artist calls lines of beauty," and he ranked our clipper ships and bridges "among the finest specimens of the *fine arts* which the world has to show." [1] Earlier in the same decade Horatio Greenough had also perceived that functionalism and honest engineering lay very close to the heart of architectural quality. But it was not until recent years that the machine became the central concern of the painter's brush. When it did so it was adopted by two very different groups of artists for quite different reasons. The first took it seriously, the second as a caustic joke.

**23**

The worship of the machine for its own sake was first promulgated by the Italian futurists, whose manifestoes of 1909 and 1910 exalted the speed and impersonal power of the airplane and the automobile and whose paintings attempted to capture the motion and force of these rather than the precision and relation of their parts. In America they had their followers in Joseph Stella and a number of other lesser-known artists who were attracted by the essentially romantic character of futurism.

Unlike the cubists and many other abstract painters, the futurists were deeply concerned with their subject matter. In New York's sky-scrapers, bridges, subways, and "els" the American members of the movement found the dynamic symbols of our machine age. Their feeling for the city was curiously linked with that of the Eight, but while the latter were exploring the intimate human aspects of New York, the former were concerned with its total impact on the senses, its pace and rhythm as a unit. Yet both approached it in an equally romantic spirit. "To realize this towering imperative vision," wrote Stella of his 1917–1918 picture, "Brooklyn Bridge," "I lived days of anxiety, torture and delight alike, trembling all over with emotion. . . Upon the swarming darkness of the night, I rung all the bells of alarm with the blaze of electricity scattered in lightnings down the oblique cables, the dynamic pillars of my composition, and to render more pungent the mystery of my metallic apparition, through the green and red glare of the signals I excavated here and there caves as subterranean passages to infernal recesses." [2]

This romantic conception of the city and the machine was shared by several painters outside the futurist group.

"I see great forces at work," wrote John Marin in a much quoted catalogue note on his early New York water colors, "great movements; the large buildings and the small buildings; the warring of the great and the small; influences of one mass on another greater or smaller mass. . . While these powers are at work pushing, pulling, sideways, downwards, upwards, I can hear the sound of their strife and there is great music being played."

It was, however, the abstract design of the machine, rather than its dynamism, which appealed to the largest group of artists both here and abroad, particularly to those like Léger in France, Belling in Germany, the Russian constructivists and, in this country, such painters as Morton Schamberg, Lyonel Feininger, Charles Demuth, Stuart Davis, and the large group known as the Immaculates. Since formal considerations predominated, it will be more logical to consider the work of these men in a later chapter. But it may be noted here that even their far less romantic approach was tinged with some of the futurists' emotion and shared, to some extent, the latter's acceptance of the machine as a symbol of modernity.

There was nothing either romantic or aesthetic in the treatment of the machine by yet another group of painters whose use of mechanical forms was only a small part of their revolutionary subject matter. These were the Dadaists and their later followers the surrealists, who turned their attention to the world of the fantastic, the irrational, and the depths of the subconscious mind. While the two movements were somewhat different in character they were both professedly anti-aesthetic and concerned with the content of their art rather than its form. Both were international movements in which Americans took some part, but neither established in this country the rather rigid organizations which, abroad, defined and maintained the "purity" of their aims. We may note for the record that Dada was officially born in Zurich in 1916, expiring about 1922, and that surrealism as a movement was announced in Paris in 1924. We will find, however, that the spirit of both was manifest in America from early in the twentieth century and perhaps even before.

The "delicious malaise" which was Dada was thought at first, writes Georges Hugnet, "to be an artistic and literary movement or a mal du siècle. But Dada was the sickness of the world," a sickness born of disillusion in the first World War, of disgust with man as a rational or moral creature, an apotheosis of futility, the accidental, the deliberately shocking and bizarre.[3]

One of the most characteristic manifestations of Dada was the conception of man as a machine without will or meaning. This had been oddly prefigured in America by what Van Wyck Brooks calls the "mechanistic philosophy" of Mark Twain, born of his private despair, which led him to refer frequently to man as "a mere coffee mill" or "sewing machine." The anti-aesthetic result of Clemens' denial of free will was also close to Dada in spirit: "Man originates nothing," he wrote, "not even a thought. . . Shakespeare could not create. He was a machine, and machines do not create." [4]

This, however, was coincidental. The machine types which became characteristic of Dada were established between 1912 and 1914, chiefly by Marcel Duchamp in Paris. His "The Bride" became the prototype of the fantastic machine with its juxtaposition of mechanical and biological forms, while his first "ready-made," an ordinary bottle rack to which he signed his name, set the type for the unaltered machine divorced from its normal function and incongruously displayed as a work of art.

These influences reached New York with the arrival of Francis Picabia in 1913 and of Duchamp himself in 1915, even before Dada was officially born. Here they found a kindred spirit in the brilliant Jewish critic and poet Benjamin De Casseres, who had already written in 1913: "Sanity and simplicity are the prime curses of civilization . . . a kind of lunacy wherein a fixed idea blankets the brain and smooths the admirable incoherence of life to a smug symmetry and proportion. . . We should mock existence at each moment, mock ourselves, mock others, mock everything by the perpetual creation of fantastic and grotesque attitudes, gestures and attributes" — a statement which might well have served as a Dada manifesto. In New York, too, a year earlier, Marius de Zayas had attacked modern art from a characteristically Dada point of view: "The modern artist is the prototype of consciousness. He works premeditatedly, he dislocates, disharmonizes, exaggerates premeditatedly. He is an eclectic in spirit and an iconoclast in action." And he concluded, as the Dadaists were to do, "Art is dead." [5]

De Casseres and de Zayas were both closely associated with Alfred Stieglitz, whose "291" gallery and whose magazine *Camera Work* had for several years been pioneering in the exhibiting and publicizing of modern art. Picabia was soon attached to the Stieglitz group (he was given an exhibition in 1913) and was active in founding another publication known as *291*, which first appeared in March 1915. For this he did a series of witty portraits in the manner of the most precise mechanical drawings. Stieglitz, being a photographer, appeared as a camera; de Zayas, the caricaturist, as a pump surmounted by a corset; Picabia himself, who was fond of racing cars, as an automobile horn. "A Young American Girl in a State of Nudity" was an unadorned drawing of a spark plug which looked suspiciously as if it had been cut from a catalogue of automobile parts.

There seems little doubt of Picabia's Dadaist intentions in these drawings, for he had earlier launched in *Camera Work* a movement called Amorphism embodied in totally blank pictures bearing only the signature Popaul Picador, an equally Dada gesture.[6] The drawings also seem closely related to Duchamp's ready-mades, which the latter continued to "produce" in this country, his most famous being the white porcelain urinal which he signed "R. Mutt" and submitted under the title "La Fontaine" to the first exhibition of the Independents in 1917.

Since Dada was not named until 1916 and was virtually unknown here before the 1920's, it is not surprising that these early manifestations by visiting Europeans were either dismissed as lunacy, as in Duchamp's case, or misinterpreted in the instance of Picabia's drawings, which were taken by Paul Haviland to embody the idea that "man has made the machine in his own image," and that "having made her superior to himself, he endows the superior beings which he conceives in his poetry and in his plastique with the qualities of machines" — a conception more in keeping with futurist philosophy and one which would later, to some extent, color the feeling of the American Immaculates.

Aside from such peripheral effects, Dada had little direct influence on American painting. Charles Demuth acknowledged a debt to Duchamp and Picabia's machines may have suggested to Morton L. Schamberg some elements in his mechanical compositions, but today the work of both these Americans seems closer to the Immaculates than to Dada. In spite of various later publications in this country such as Duchamp's *the blind man* and *Wrong-Wrong* or Picabia's and Walter Arensberg's *391*, Dada attracted only one distinguished American follower, the painter and photographer Man Ray, much of whose life was spent in Paris where he produced without the use of a camera his extraordinary "rayographs." With Duchamp, Man Ray published in America in 1921 one issue of *New York Dada*, which claimed Rube Goldberg as a kindred spirit for his cartoons of complex and miraculous gadgets. An article "Pug Debs Make Society Bow" also implicated the painters Marsden Hartley and Joseph Stella, although there is no evidence that their work was ever affected by the movement. They may have flirted with it as the sculptor Archipenko did in the same year when he designed a witty advertisement in *The Arts* for the "ARCHIE PEN CO." [7]

Perhaps Dada's truest exponents in this country, however, were men who were totally unaware of the existence of such a movement, but who were sensitive in their own way to the general disillusion which followed the war. Charles Burchfield, discharged from the army in 1919, wrote later of his work at this time: "There followed a period of degeneracy in my art that I have never been able to explain. . . I later destroyed all the painting of this period . . . viewed from any angle whatsoever, there is not a single redeeming feature about them — and I may add that the vagaries of the Da-da school were nothing compared to mine at this time, though I had never heard of Da-daism then." [8]

The same spirit gave birth to an obscure movement, largely forgotten since nothing was ever written concerning it, but remarkably similar to Dada in some respects. Founded by Holger Cahill about 1920, even its name, Inje-Inje, had something of the same nonsensical cadence as Dada though it bore more significance in relation to the purpose of the movement.

*Inje*, Cahill had read in a book by a Fellow of the Royal Geographical Society, was the only word in the language of a South American tribe of Indians, who managed however to communicate a wide range of meanings through different inflections of the word accompanied by various gestures. His movement proposed to return the arts to a comparable simplicity, to cut away the superstructure of our cultural refinements and discover the basic and most direct forms of human expression. Painting, for instance, was to be reduced primarily to horizontal and vertical forms, though not in as rigid a manner as the Dutch painters of *De Stijl* evolved nor even necessarily abstract.

Insofar as Inje-Inje proposed a serious aesthetic program it was contrary to the spirit of Dada and more closely related to the cubists' earlier rediscovery of primitive art. But Inje-Inje was only half, or perhaps three-quarters, serious. Bizarre and deliberately shocking elements gave a true Dada flavor to many of Cahill's proposals. Concerts were planned using only percussion instruments such as African signal drums and a primitive Philippine "flute" with a range of two notes when struck on the wrist. Theatrical performances were to have been presented by actors in blank masks, nude except for mitts and a G string.

Inje-Inje lasted for only two or three years and had relatively little effect on American painting, although Mark Tobey and Alfred Maurer were both involved, William Gropper and John Sloan to a lesser extent. Frank Overton Colbert, a Chickasaw Indian, was one of the most active painters in the group. Robert Henri was opposed but is said to have told Sloan later that there was perhaps something in it. Several Inje-Inje poems were written by Malcolm Cowley and Orrick Johns, but there were never funds for the projected magazine and most of Cahill's program was unrealized. Nevertheless it remains one of the most significant manifestations of postwar unrest in this country, its mixture of constructive and destructive elements more characteristic of America's underlying optimism than was the more thoroughly nihilistic spirit of Dada.

Dada died officially in Europe in 1922, but many of its features reappeared in surrealism, which was announced by André Breton in Paris two years later. The relation of the two movements has been most succinctly stated by Alfred Barr: "The Surrealists preserved the

**29**

anti-rational character of Dada but developed a far more systematic and serious experimental attitude toward the subconscious as the essential source of art." We may also recall Breton's definition of surrealism: "Pure psychic automatism, by which it is intended to express, verbally, in writing or by other means, the real process of thought. It is thought's dictation, all exercise of reason and every esthetic or moral preoccupation being absent." [9] The mockery of Dada was hushed, but its anti-aesthetic bias as well as its irrationality were perpetuated.

No art movement in history has so systematically rifled the past, partly to discover motivating material, partly to establish historical evidence in support of its thesis. In America the surrealists soon claimed Edgar Allan Poe, with some justification, as a forerunner of their spirit. With much less reason they also found a link with the nineteenth-century painter William M. Harnett, whose *trompe l'oeil* still lifes Edouard Roditi described (parodying lines by Lautréamont often quoted by surrealists) as "beautiful as the fortuitous encounter, on an old door panel, of a horse-shoe and a newspaper clipping." Disregarding the fact that two of the three paintings illustrating these remarks were not by Harnett, this kind of argument, like much surrealist research, seems of dubious value since it ignores the fact that the apparently mysterious combinations of objects by Harnett and his circle were often no more profound than pictorial puns or sly anecdotes in paint.[10]

In spite of such questionable judgments, one cannot deny that the spirit of surrealism, with its probing of the depths in the subconscious mind, did exist in this country long before the movement itself was born. De Casseres, whom we have already quoted in a proto-Dada spirit, was more consistently surrealist in his sentiments. Writing for Stieglitz's *Camera Work* in 1911–1912 (and hence doubtless read by many of the young artists who exhibited at 291), he emphasized repeatedly the part of instinct in creative expression: "Consciousness in art is only the antenna of the blind unknowable Force and intelligence is only its nerve. . . Imagination is the dream of the Unconscious. It is the realm of the gorgeous, monstrous hallucinations of the Unconscious. It is the hasheesh of genius. . . I desire," he concluded, "to be ephemeral, protean, and to chase the dazzling butterflies of my fancy across abyss and meadowland and even into those fatal caves in the moon where the Goddess of Lunacy spins her cataleptic dreams." [11]

Stieglitz himself seems to have been briefly affected by De Casseres' mood; at least he published a few years later his "One Hour's Sleep — Three Dreams," macabre and erotic visions of his own death and "The Woman." [12] But none of his artists nor indeed any others seem to have felt the same impulse. For while we had then, as always, a number of painters who lived in a visionary world of the imagination, such as Ryder, Eilshemius, and Davies, their dreams were romantic, idyllic, and we might say less self-consciously unconscious than those of Stieglitz or De Casseres.

Even when the paintings of the orthodox surrealists of Paris were finally exhibited in America, which was not until 1930–1931, there were few wholehearted converts to the movement. The American, Man Ray, was a member of the Paris group and in this country Joseph Cornell incorporated surrealist elements in his fantastic arrangements which were also, perhaps, related to the machines of Dada. During the 1930's surrealist influence was also apparent in the work of several younger artists such as Peter Blume, Knud Merrild, Walter Quirt, Wallace Putnam, and Federico Castellón, but was so modified in most cases by their formal interests that their work can best be discussed elsewhere.

There is no doubt that the movement has strengthened its influence during the last decade due to the settling here (in some cases permanently) of several foreign-born surrealists, among them Yves Tanguy, William Stanley Hayter, and Matta Echaurren, all of whom arrived in 1939, Salvador Dali who came in 1940, and Max Ernst in 1941. Concurrently, more Americans have adopted elements of surrealism, which will be found, in realist guise, in the painting of Louis Guglielmi, John Atherton, and Alton Pickens, and, in abstract form, in the work of a large group including Arshile Gorky, William Baziotes, Boris Margo, Gerome Kamrowski, and Jackson Pollock. But again few of these can be called orthodox surrealists. Only a very occasional figure, like Dorothea Tanning, has worked consistently within the hallucinatory realm of traditional surrealism.

Why has the movement, while enriching the art of so many of our

**31**

younger painters, failed to attract more wholehearted support here? Perhaps the chief reason lies in our traditions and background. "No author, without a trial," said Hawthorne in his preface to *The Marble Faun*, "can conceive of the difficulty of writing a romance about a country where there is no shadow, no antiquity, no mystery, no picturesque and gloomy wrong, nor anything but a commonplace prosperity in broad and simple daylight, as is happily the case with my dear native land." Plainly this is not an atmosphere congenial to the dark dreams of surrealism.

"His art," writes Robert Motherwell of the surrealist painter Max Ernst, "depends on a sense of the vicious past. To the American mind nothing could be more alien. . . Such images as a black mass, a bloody nun, an invader from the east cannot arouse deep feelings in most of us . . . for better or worse most Americans have no sensation of being either elevated or smothered by the past. . . Consciously abandoning the past is the essentially American creative act; we painters here remain indifferent to the objects surrounding us. Our emotional interest is not in the external world, but in creating a world of our own. . . It is from this reasoning that we can account for the fact that objectless painting, that is, various modes of abstraction, appeals more to most modern American painters than surrealism." [13]

This is stated from the abstract artist's point of view, but with slight changes it would probably represent also the attitude of many American painters who *are* interested "in the external world." Alton Pickens may paint an acrobat with his head sprouting incongruously from his crotch, but his "fantasy of distortion," while doubtless owing something to surrealism, is based primarily, to use his own words, "on the every-day existence of the people around me." [14] Like some of Guglielmi's art, it is social commentary heightened in effect by surrealist touches.

All of these painters and many more have made serious use of surrealism, which has provided them with a new means of expressing those intangible parts of human experience which lie deep in the atavistic layers of the mind. But it is perhaps also characteristic of our skeptical and irreverent spirit that we have occasionally found something a little ridiculous in the movement's excessive concern with black magic and its determined effort, as it often seems, to dredge up from the subconscious the most grotesquely unpleasant aspects of human thought. This attitude has been reflected in the weird and libidinous drawings of James Thurber, Richard Taylor, Saul Steinberg, and a number of other "cartoonists" (the term seems inappropriate) whose work has been published largely in the *New Yorker*. For them, even while they make fun of it, surrealism seems to have had a kind of repellent fascination. It has also cast a more obvious spell on the commercial artist and the window dresser whose perennial search for novelty has discovered in its superficial aspects a gratifying mine of arresting oddities and elegant eroticism.

Surrealism, in short, has colored a rather large part of our modern art in the last decade and while it has not established an organized movement here, its influence continues to be strong.

## 4

## REVOLUTION IN FORM

### expressionism

When Arthur Jerome Eddy published in America in 1914 his *Cubists and Post-Impressionists*, he dedicated it "to that spirit the beating of whose restless wings is heard in every land." This was a romantic but apt description of the two great formal revolutions in the arts, expressionism and abstractionism, which, from their international beginnings in France and Germany, have swept through the western world abrogating and altering though not destroying the representational basis on which the arts had rested since the Renaissance.

In America this revolution was more radical than abroad for we had had no Cézannes, no Gauguins, Van Goghs, or Seurats to prepare the way and point the evolutionary nature of the change. We had even lagged sadly in our knowledge of these painters and by 1900 were just beginning to accept without reservations the impressionism of Monet, Pissarro, and our own men. Yet American artists had a part in forming the expressionist and abstract movements from almost the beginning, and these have gradually acclimated themselves in the United States until they now flourish here with perhaps more vigor than abroad. Like surrealism, but to a far greater extent, they have colored many of our traditional art forms and have in turn been somewhat altered by the latter — a process of repeated cross influences.

Of the two movements, expressionism has probably had the larger and more continuous, though less radical, effect on our art. In tracing its growth we shall use the term rather loosely to indicate all art which depends on free and obvious distortions of natural forms to convey emotional feeling. There is also an abstract expressionism which achieves

**34**

similar romantic intensity by the disruption of geometric forms. But this is so closely linked to the development of abstract art that we shall consider it as a phase of the latter.

Of the two main strands of European expressionism, that developed in Germany about 1905 by the group called *Die Brücke* had at the beginning a relatively small influence on our art. In the same year, however, a group of French expressionists, led by Henri Matisse, had come to public attention at the Salon d'Automne where their joint exhibit had won them the name of *les fauves* or "the wild beasts." Within five years this group, and especially Matisse, had noticeably affected American artists and public both here and abroad.

The first Matisse exhibition in America was held at Alfred Stieglitz's 291 Gallery in 1908, the same year in which the Eight had offended the conservative with their social realism. The more radical innovations of the French artist, which seemed to strike at the very foundations of art, bewildered and enraged the critics. Even one of the most sympathetic voices, while granting that he was " a great artist if estimated from the brilliant stroke, the subtle elimination and the interesting composition," was forced to conclude, "But Matisse, like nearly all the other very modern Frenchmen, feels that pull toward physical distortion, that sickening, malevolent desire to present the nude (especially women) so vulgarized, so hideously at odds with nature as to suggest, in spite of the technical mastery of his art, first of all the loathsome and the abnormal, and both with a marvel of execution and a bewildering cleverness that somehow fills one with a distaste for art and life." [1]

Within the next few years, however, several American critics took the opportunity to visit the Fauves in their own studios and to report courageously on being at least partially converted to the new art. Charles Caffin called on Matisse in 1909, discussed the relation of his paintings to the primitive African sculpture which he found in his studio, and when the initial shock had worn off, "I found that after I had been with his pictures for some time, they exerted a spell upon my imagination. So much so, that after I had left them I could not immediately look at 'ordinary' pictures." Gelett Burgess had much the same experience in 1910. "If you can imagine," he wrote of his first impression of the Fauves at the Salon des Indépendants, "what a particularly sanguinary little girl of eight, half crazed with gin, would do to a white-washed wall, if left alone with a box of crayons, then you will come near to fancying what most of this work was like." But he, too, talked with the painters in their studios, discussed their aims, looked again at their pictures and concluded, "They are in earnest and do stand for a serious revolt. . . There is, moreover, something . . . virile . . . ecstatic about their work," which he reassured Americans was not in any sense degenerate as they were being daily told.[2]

At about the same time a number of young American artists studying in Paris were attracted to the new movement. One of them, Max Weber, helped to organize a class taught by Matisse which started in the fall of 1907. Two Americans attended the first season, Weber and Arthur Burdett Frost, Jr., and others soon followed. Patrick Henry Bruce, who had met Matisse through the Steins about 1908, was for some time thereafter *massier* of the class. Arthur B. Carles seems to have been there briefly and Morgan Russell was also one of his students.

But Matisse exerted more influence through his work than through his teaching. In class he insisted on rigorous training in draftsmanship and discouraged his pupils from becoming Fauves overnight. Russell, for instance, has said that though he studied with him he "never adopted his manner," [3] and the influence on Bruce was also slight. On the other hand, Matisse was emulated for a time quite closely by Alfred Maurer, Morton L. Schamberg, William Zorach, James H. Daugherty, and Eduard (now Edward) Steichen, all of whom were in Paris during the first dozen years of the century.

Many of these painters were friends, meeting each other and the French moderns at the home of Gertrude and Leo Stein, who were then forming their impressive collection of modern art. They even had their own organization, though it does not seem to have functioned very actively, in the New Society of American Artists in Paris which seceded in 1908 from the older and more conservative Society of American Artists in Paris. Among its members were Weber, Maurer, and Bruce; also Steichen who, in addition to his own painting and photography, was helping Stieglitz assemble exhibitions of modern art to be shown at 291.

**36**

If few memorable pictures resulted from all this early activity centering around Matisse it is scarcely surprising for nearly all these artists were still young, indeed still in their student days. Much of their work was thinly derivative, as student effort is likely to be, but here and there an artist assimilated the new influences and produced mature and personal statements. Alfred Maurer, slightly older than the others and already a successful academic painter before his conversion to modernism, was one of these. Another, perhaps the best, was Max Weber who, before turning to cubism, painted several predominantly Fauve pictures like "Decoration with Cloud" in which the nervously attenuated human figures are both expressive and quite individual.

Matisse was the central influence, but the more conservative Fauvism of Derain and Marquet also had its effect, particularly on two American artists whose early careers followed for a short time the same path. Bernard Karfiol and Samuel Halpert both commenced their studies in Paris in 1901–1902 at the usual academic schools, the former at the Academie Julian, the latter at the Beaux-Arts. Both soon became interested in the modern movement, knew its leaders personally, and adapted the more conservative style of Derain to their own ends. Karfiol also added elements of Picasso's rose and blue periods, while Halpert was strongly influenced for a time by Delaunay's dynamic architectural studies of St. Severin Cathedral. The art of both helped greatly to popularize modernism in America where it was more easily understood and more quickly appreciated than that of Maurer or Weber, both of whom were vilified in the American press for many years.

It was still another pair of American painters who made, it now seems, the most independent use of Fauve and cubist elements, although in both cases their expressionist work was apart from the main line of their development and had little influence on others. Both Charles Demuth and Lyonel Feininger had early contacts with European modernism, but both incorporated many other elements in their highly personal styles. The water colors which Demuth did in the years immediately following his return from France in 1914 and the illustrations and paintings which Feininger did in the years 1906–1912 are quite different in some respects and entirely independent of each other. Yet in the work of both there is the same free and supple patterning in flat areas which overlap, sometimes almost like collage; there is also a fanciful and imaginative quality in their work which sets it apart from the heavier style of most expressionism. Here the similarity ends, for Demuth's work is aloof, subtle, and aristocratic; it often struck his contemporaries as morbid — particularly his illustrations for Henry James's *The Turn of the Screw*. Feininger's ragged and more vigorous patterns translated the contemporary scene into a world of gothic fantasy peopled by characters and buildings of improbable proportions. In this respect his work was perhaps closer to the early paintings of yet another pioneer American expressionist, Ben Benn, whose flatly decorative figure paintings of about 1915 were also reminiscent of folk tale and legend, though more in the Chagall and Campendonk vein of peasant art.

Feininger had settled in Germany but the expressionism of that country had much less effect on his art than it did on that of several other young Americans who studied there in the years before the war. One of the first to arrive was Albert Bloch who came to Munich in 1909 and was early associated with the Blaue Reiter group of modern painters. While much of his work was semi-abstract and strongly influenced by the decorative style of Franz Marc, he also painted some rather sensitive expressionist portraits and in one picture, his "Scene from a Pantomime" of 1914, apparently attempted to translate an abstract painting by Kandinsky into representational terms.[4] More consistently expressionist was the work of Oscar Bluemner, who in 1912 gave up a successful career as a New York architect to study painting in Germany (where he had been born) and elsewhere in Europe. Out of both French and German sources he evolved a style of strong color and romantically patterned structure which later was to approach, as we shall see, certain other romantic phases of American art.

Meanwhile, in the "House of the Great Garlic Stench," as De Casseres called America, modern art, both native and European, was virtually unknown outside the small circle which frequented Stieglitz's

291. This was abruptly changed by the Armory Show of 1913, which had an immediate effect on many young American painters. Cézanne and the cubists outweighed at first the influence of Matisse and the Fauves, but expressionism grew steadily, nevertheless, in the years following the exhibition, developing along personal lines rather than those of any school or group.

Among the early leaders in the movement were several men who had experimented with abstract art but who abandoned it before 1920 to become expressionists in a representational vein. Chief of these were Max Weber and Marsden Hartley; another, who was to have for a time an even greater influence on our art, was Thomas Benton. The three were totally dissimilar except in their general use of free distortions for romantic ends.

From about 1917 Weber began to form his mature style, colored with strong religious and racial (Jewish) feeling. Lloyd Goodrich, in his sensitive appraisal of the artist's work at this time, has pointed out that for Weber from now on "the emotional content [of his pictures] was so compelling that it dictated the style, causing him to give up abstract stylization and to speak directly and simply." [5] This did not mean naturalistically. Weber's figures are always emotionally expressive, now ecstatically elongated, now squat and heavy with a monumental repose which might seem more classical than romantic, if the twist of a hand or a head did not establish, nearly always, underlying emotional tensions.

Weber's art has been so very personal and so intimately connected with his racial feelings that it has not proved very adaptable to others. This makes it no less important in its own right, but less so as a fertilizing agent in American painting. In the case of Marsden Hartley it has been otherwise. "Personal art," he once wrote, "is for me a matter of spiritual indelicacy." [6] The broader, more generalized emotional content in his work and the simple, angular rhythms of his style have influenced large numbers of younger painters. Like Weber, Hartley began to lose interest in abstraction about 1917 and by 1919 had returned entirely to representational work. Admiring the romantic visions of Ryder and the realism of Homer, influenced by both French and German expressionism, Hartley rather miraculously developed out of these and other divergent sources the strong, astringent style which reflected so purely, in spite of his reticence, the artist's poetic feeling for the rugged New England landscape and its people.

A third and again quite different strand in our expressionist art was spun at about the same time by Thomas Hart Benton. Like the others, Benton experimented, though less wholeheartedly, with abstraction, which he pursued at least to 1916 when he wrote that he believed "the representation of objective forms and the presentation of abstract ideas to be of equal value." [7] In a remarkably consistent stylistic development he early translated the flamelike distortions of Tintoretto and El Greco into a simplified modern idiom which served admirably to express the romantic dynamism with which he viewed American life. His later antimodern philosophy and his occasional excursions into a more sober realism cannot obscure the fact that he has contributed to our art a fluent kind of expressionism, vigorous if rather insensitive. His influence, however, has operated chiefly on the romantic realists who have found the less extreme elements of his style more in keeping with his and their regionalist aims.

During the twenties and early thirties American expressionism grew, slowly at first, then with increasing rapidity. Again it is difficult to see any dominant trends within the general confines of the movement. The men whom we have just discussed seem now to have been clearly its leading figures, but they had not then won their eventual recognition and their influence in the 1920's was still small. For some time expressionism was to remain a movement of many personal experiments and we can only touch briefly on some of those who contributed to its growth.

Like the earlier men, Paul Burlin had worked in a semi-abstract manner, which he had apparently developed independently in Taos. This he began to inform with strongly expressionist feeling in his murals for the home of George A. Harris, done shortly before he left America in 1921 for an eleven-year stay abroad. There he shed the cubist overtones which persist in the Harris murals and developed his purely expressionist mature style. Another convert of about this time was Benjamin Kopman whose protean art has been swayed by many influences from Ryder to Rouault, though maintaining through its changes an emotional quality that is both a little heavy and exotic.

The attachment of many of our expressionists to subjects which have for them a special emotional significance is rather characteristic of the movement. Weber's long concern with Jewish religious rites, Benton's with rural America, and Hartley's eventual concentration on the coast of Maine are cases in point. A deep seriousness of mood has also marked much of our expressionist art, but this has been belied by several American painters. Yasuo Kuniyoshi's work of the 1920's combined fantasy and sensuality in nervous decorative patterns quite different from the heavier rhythms of the early men. While Kuniyoshi drew in succession on a number of recognizable sources such as Campendonk and Chagall and, later, Pascin, his art was more truly exotic than any of these in its odd wedding of Oriental and modern Occidental vision. Later it was to lose much of its playfulness and some of its Oriental qualities, gaining in compensation a greater depth of feeling. But from at least 1922 on it was, as Lloyd Goodrich has pointed out, "among the most original products of the modern movement." [8]

Expressionism, as embodied in the work of these men, was a private and an extremely personal way of painting. But it also became at this time a tool for social comment and a formidable weapon in the hands of several artists who were concerned with the struggle for social justice. "We painters for the People," said William Gropper, "must not only tell them the truth in human justice and righteousness but . . . we must say it better and with more conviction than anyone else in order to be accepted." [9] For this purpose expressionism emerged, by the early 1930's, as a more forceful language than had been the romantic realism of Higgins and Luks.

Gropper himself was one of the first in this development. Starting as a cartoonist, he took up painting in the 1920's and carried into it something of the caricaturist's tendency to perpetuate exaggerated types of humanity, rather than to invent anew from picture to picture. In his graphic work, however, he has shown a constant satirical incisiveness. Ben Shahn started also in somewhat the same vein when he recalled, in 1931–1932, the bitter disillusion of liberals in the outcome of the Sacco and Vanzetti trial. His remarkable series of gouaches on this subject are more restrained and deeper in feeling than much socially conscious art. But already Shahn was moving away from expressionism toward a different style which we must consider elsewhere.

Much of our expressionist art devoted to social reform, being inspired by a cause which seemed at times lost or hopelessly beyond reach, has been exceptionally bitter. Among the first to strike this note was the German-born painter and caricaturist George Grosz, who settled here in 1932, became an American citizen and one of our most powerful expressionist painters. Grosz has never been enlisted in the cause of labor, but among his early work here was a group of satirical water colors attacking middle-class materialism, as he had done in Germany, with an intensity which made it appear not stupid and pretentious but unspeakably ugly and obscene.

Something of the same weird and repellent quality has informed the work of Philip Evergood, although he has made it serve rather different ends than Grosz, using it only occasionally to caricature the wealthy. His interest has lain more consistently in demonstrating the terrible and wasting effects of poverty, war, and all forms of oppression on the human body and the human spirit. His victims are sometimes heroic with a boisterous unconcern for consequences; more often they are warped and twisted out of normal human semblance. His acid, arbitrary color and his startling distortions of form are typically expressionist, but with these he occasionally mixes a precise realism like that of the *neue Sachlichkeit* movement in Germany which, in both his "private" and his "social" paintings, intensifies the mood of wild and forcibly restrained emotions.

From the middle 1930's to the present, expressionism has spread so widely through our art that it is impossible to do more than indicate some of its phases. In this period nearly all the painters we have mentioned reached their full maturity and produced their finest work. Of the more important figures, only Maurer had died earlier (in 1932) leaving as perhaps the most complete expression of his tragic career the somber "Self-Portrait with Hat" done about 1927-1928.

Weber reached the peak of his expressionist phase, in representational form, about 1940 when he painted the religious ecstasy of the "Hasidic Dance" and the same year found Hartley transforming the thunder of the Maine surf into one of his most ample and majestic canvases, "The Lighthouse." The second World War had its effect on Kuniyoshi in the melancholy symbolism of "Headless Horse Who Wants to Jump," but he had also recaptured, after going through a more naturalistic phase, the imaginative fantasy which seems his most personal note. It was the war, too, which returned George Grosz from sensuous nudes and idyllic Cape Cod landscapes to the most powerful of all his nightmare visions of the plight of humanity in the modern world.

In the same period a host of younger artists and some older ones have explored the traditional forms of expressionism and devised a number of new ones. Among these, Franklin C. Watkins stands out as one of the most original talents. While he has drawn on many European sources from El Greco to Van Gogh, the traces of these are hardly perceptible in the vigorous and dramatic subjects, such as "Suicide in Costume," "Soliloquy," and "The Fire Eater," which earned him his sudden reputation in the early 1930's. Now massive, now attenuated, his forceful distortions were individual, disciplined, and closely related to the mood of his subjects. Later, Watkins' art became more reserved and also more sensitive as he turned increasingly to portraits and still lifes, but very recently, in a pair of religious murals commissioned by Henry P. McIlhenny, he has again taken up subjects of more dramatic scope.

As Central European expressionism became better known here, its influence and the allied one of Marsden Hartley have affected in a general way the work of many painters such as Joseph De Martini, Everett Spruce, Lamar Dodd, John Heliker, and Ben-Zion. Theirs has been largely a landscape art, but the figure style of certain German ex-

**43**

pressionists, particularly Max Beckmann, has also had its influence on painters like Carlos Lopez and on many young students during Beckmann's brief teaching career in the United States.

Much of our expressionism, however, is both more individual and, in a sense, more eclectic, mixing freely elements drawn from the Germans, from Rouault and Soutine in France, and from the Mexicans Orozco and Siqueiros, as well as from native sources. Boston was for a time the center of this line of development, due in part to the presence there of two influential teachers, Dr. Denman Ross and, later, Karl Zerbe; due even more to the accidents of emigration which brought to Boston the families of three young painters of Baltic-Jewish origin, Jack Levine, Hyman Bloom, and David Aronson. Zerbe, though German born, had worked in both France and Mexico before he started teaching in Boston in 1938. His art, a little colder and more reserved than most expressionism, revived an interest in the expressive use of surface textures and pioneered in the exploration of certain technical problems such as the use of encaustic, the old but largely abandoned wax medium. Of the younger trio, Aronson was his pupil. Levine and Bloom studied with Ross, whose color theories and wide knowledge of art did much to help them find their way to their individual styles, though Ross was not, himself, an exponent of expressionism.

Levine and Bloom were mature artists by the middle 1930's; the much younger Aronson did not begin to paint independently until nearly ten years later. Yet the early work of all three shows a certain similarity, particularly in its strong debt to a Rouault-Soutine influence, which appeared both in the character of the distortions and in the richly crusted color. Thereafter, they developed along different and entirely individual lines. Levine's art has gained in power with more restraint and has found its vein in macabre humor and a social satire sharper than any except Evergood's. Bloom has moved in a more mystical direction which found expression first in his religious pictures and since then in an extraordinary series depicting human putrefaction and decay. These link curiously with several others tracing the riddles of time and meaning in archaeological remains. Aronson, employing, as he wrote,

**44**

"the gentle and the grotesque in the same picture," has produced an impressive group of softly lyrical religious subjects.[10]

This kind of expressionism, which might be called humanistic because of its deep preoccupation with spiritual and psychological values and its use in general of organic rather than angular distortions, was not limited to Boston but has appeared spontaneously elsewhere. Mitchell Siporin has used it in his own fashion for social comment, while Rico Lebrun and Darrel Austin have pushed it, in quite different ways, close to the bounds of surrealism. Abraham Rattner, carrying its distortions even further, has given it a lyrical turn, largely by his glowing color. And we must admit that in the hands of many lesser artists it has become at times a turgid and exclamatory style which professes emotions that are more melodramatic than real.

Oddly, expressionism has not had nearly as large a following among our sculptors as our painters, perhaps because the former were for many years absorbed in the technical-aesthetic problems of direct carving which ran counter, in some degree, to the free distortions demanded by expressionism. Except for the portrait busts of Jacob Epstein, who was living constantly abroad, little expressionist sculpture of moment was produced in this country until the decades of the thirties and forties, and even in these years it has been in the minority as far as representational work is concerned. Two women, Lu Duble and Minna Harkavy, have done perhaps the best and most consistent work of this kind — the former in vigorously distorted figures much influenced by the German carver Barlach, the latter in a more restrained and individual vein which often escapes, however, into a style that might better be described as romantic realism. Among others who have explored expressionism for a time are Randolph W. Johnston, Nathaniel Kaz, Berta Margoulies, Charles Umlauf, Nat Werner, and Anita Weschler. But several of these have turned already in other directions, and our total body of expressionist sculpture, except in abstract form, remains small.

# 5

## REVOLUTION IN FORM

### abstract art, 1910-1930

There can be small doubt that the most radical revolution which ever took place in American art is that which centered in the international abstract movement. Twice before 1930 it erupted in this country; twice its opponents proclaimed it dead. But again in the 1940's it became a dominant mode of expression, more varied, original, and widespread than in either of its earlier phases.

Every writer on the subject has deplored the inaccurate connotation of the word "abstract" as a general description of nonrepresentational art, but most have ended by using it. Without arguing the question again, we shall also accept its popular meaning as a definition of all art which does not represent the objective world in recognizable form but either rearranges it in arbitrary compositions or substitutes purely formal patterns invented by the artist without reference to nature (insofar as that is possible).

In Europe abstract art had started in Paris about 1906 with the early experiments of the cubists, spread rapidly to Germany where Kandinsky painted what is probably the first purely abstract picture in 1910, and appeared almost simultaneously in Italy, Russia, and Holland, taking somewhat different forms in each. While it did not reach America on a large scale until the time of the Armory Show in 1913, many American artists took part in its development abroad from very nearly the beginning, and one, Maurice Prendergast, developed even before the French cubists a strongly patterned semi-abstract style, based partly on his knowledge of Cézanne — a style which may well claim to be the earliest "modern" and proto-abstract one in this country.

It is not necessary here to review the shifting emphasis which the many European "isms" gave to abstraction, but it is important to note that in general the movement followed two divergent paths, one classical, rational, and intellectual, the other romantic, intuitive, and emotional. As Alfred Barr has pointed out, both stemmed from French impressionism. The first developed through Cézanne's simplification of forms to the balanced, geometrical art of the cubists and the various Russian and Dutch constructivist movements. The second was given its direction by Gauguin and his circle, followed by the Fauvism of Matisse; it appeared in the abstract expressionism of Kandinsky's prewar work and later in the amorphous or nongeometrical forms of the abstract surrealists.[1]

There was, however, a third kind of abstract art which had, at the beginning, the largest influence on American painters. This was represented in Italy by futurism, in Paris by Orphism, two movements quite different in some respects but alike in their attempt to infuse an essentially romantic dynamism into the classical forms of the cubists. Like sixteenth-century mannerism, which had also tried to breathe romantic feeling into the classical formula of the High Renaissance, this uneasy alliance did not last long abroad. But in America, as we shall see, it developed some surprisingly original and vigorous forms.

As with expressionism, the pioneer American abstractionists were mostly young students working abroad in the years immediately following the public debut of cubism in Paris in 1908. A landscape done by Arthur G. Dove in that year is said to have some cubist form in the trees; [2] if so Dove was probably the first to feel the new influence. By about 1910 he had been joined by Max Weber, Abraham Walkowitz, and Konrad Cramer. By the time of the Armory Show in 1913, Henry L. McFee, John Marin, Morgan Russell, Stanton Macdonald-Wright, Frederick R. Shaler, Joseph Stella, Marsden Hartley, Lyonel Feininger, Preston Dickinson, Morton L. Schamberg, Charles Sheeler, and possibly a few others had also begun to work in an abstract or semi-abstract way. In the two or three years after the Armory Show many others were attracted, among them Patrick Henry Bruce, Walter Pach, John R. Covert, A. S. Baylinson, Charles H. Walther, Man Ray, Georgia

O'Keeffe, A. B. Frost, Jr., William Zorach, and Stuart Davis. Andrew
M. Dasburg and Arthur B. Carles probably belong in this group although they may have done some abstract work earlier.

The exact chronology of the movement is less important, however,
than the kind of abstract art which these men fashioned and its relation
to their European sources. Cubism, which started by reducing forms to
their simplest geometrical essence and ended by taking nature apart and
reassembling it in flat patterns of logically ordered beauty, had few
direct followers among the Americans. Only one, Max Weber, seems
today of lasting importance; several of the cubist pictures which he
did between 1910 and 1919, however, are among the most successful
early abstractions produced in this country. At the beginning, Weber's
work derived perhaps too closely from the primitive cubism of Picasso,
but within a few years he had developed a massive, brooding style of his
own, as in his "Geranium" of 1911. There are strong Fauvist overtones
in the latter but Weber returned, between 1915 and 1919, to a more
purely cubist style in such pictures as "The Chinese Restaurant" and
"The Visit" which, in spite of their relation to the rococo phase of the
French movement, are highly individual pictures. In addition to Weber,
Henry L. McFee experimented briefly with abstract art about 1911–
1912 and has said that "cubism, to me, was the principal interest," [3] and
William Zorach, about 1917, painted several pictures which were close
to synthetic cubism. But neither of these pursued their work beyond
an experimental stage, and Weber stands alone as the one pioneer
American cubist of stature.

The truth is that American art, which had been predominantly romantic and realist for over a hundred years, found pure cubism too
classical and intellectual to be readily assimilated. This attitude is reflected in even the sympathetic criticism of the day. "It may be," wrote
Eddy of the cubists in 1914, "the manner they have chosen is so abstract,
so scientifically theoretical, that it will in the end — if pursued — kill
the imagination [and] stifle all delight." "The Post-cubists are now in
the fore-front of the movement for true art," thought John Weichsel,
but they "have taken his [man's] logical faculty as a starting point — a

fatal procedure," and "have transgressed the boundary of art and en-croached upon science and artistry."[4]

In Paris meantime, two small groups, one European, the other American, were evolving almost simultaneously a modified cubism which was to have a somewhat greater appeal in this country. In the years 1909–1911 Robert Delaunay (whose earlier studies of St. Severin had influenced Samuel Halpert) mixed cubism with his dynamic style by exploding a cubist bomb, so to speak, under the Eiffel Tower and recording on several canvases the fragmentation and the wild motion which this produced. Pursuing his experiments into total abstraction, he developed in 1912–1913 (with Frank Kupka) an art of brilliantly colored disks which seemed to recede or advance according to the recessive qualities of the different colors used. Orphism, as Guillaume Apollinaire called the movement, differed from orthodox cubism in two important respects: it was totally abstract and its departure from the cubists' muted color set up a dynamic motion in depth which was absent from the flat and static patterns of the former.

Almost precisely the same results were achieved a few months later by two young Americans, Morgan Russell and Stanton Macdonald-Wright, who called their movement Synchromism and waged a sharp battle of manifestoes against the Orphists. It is difficult now to see any real difference between the abstract work of the two movements. The Synchromists also painted disks and other geometrical forms in colors which retreated or advanced in space, and, while they claimed that "with us the quality of depth provokes a subjective emotion,"[5] the same might be said of the Orphists. In addition to their pure abstractions, both Russell and Macdonald-Wright continued to do semi-abstract work in which they applied to still lifes and the human figure the same dynamic color structure.

As an organized movement Synchromism did not survive the war, although Macdonald-Wright continued to work in this vein until 1920 and Morgan Russell, who lived abroad in quiet retirement until 1946, has never entirely given it up. But its greatest influence was exerted in the period of about 1913–1916 when it was actively publicized by its cofounders and especially by their highly partisan supporter Willard

**49**

Huntington Wright, who told the world that Gauguin was a "poseur," Van Gogh a "crazy Dutchman . . . buried for all time," the cubists "pretty and superficial," futurism "a passing noise," but that Synchromism "seems destined to have the most far-reaching effects of any art force since Cézanne." [6]

While its influence was not quite so sweeping, it did indeed attract a number of other young Americans both here and abroad. In Paris Thomas Benton met Macdonald-Wright and tried for a time to combine Synchromism with classic compositions, but the results, which he exhibited at the Forum Exhibition in 1916, did not satisfy him and he soon gave it up. At the same exhibition Andrew Dasburg showed an abstract "Improvisation" in which, he said, "my intention has been to coordinate color and contour into a phantastic of form," by using "colors which, by their depressive or stimulating qualities, approach or recede in accordance with . . . the rhythmic scheme of the picture," a completely Synchromist aim. In addition to their large 1913 exhibitions in Munich and Paris, the Synchromists had held a New York show at the Carroll Gallery in the same year; this may have influenced the exhibition at the MacDowell Club, also in 1913, which Willard Huntington Wright condemned as a feeble imitation.[7] It may also have been seen by Henry L. McFee who has said that in addition to his cubist researches he was also experimenting "in abstract painting and in giving color its proper place in space." [8]

Two other young Americans seem to have worked in much the same vein, but under the direct influence of French Orphism rather than Synchromism. Patrick Henry Bruce, born in Virginia in 1881, had studied with Henri in New York in 1902–1903 and in the latter year had gone to Paris where he lived until a few months before his death in 1937. For several years he had worked independently, much influenced by Cézanne and Renoir, and about 1908, as we have seen, had entered the Matisse class. Early in 1914 he began to paint abstractly, somewhat in the manner of Delaunay, and in the next three or four years he turned out a series of large "Compositions" in which the brilliant colors, roughly applied with a palette knife, establish massive, dynamic rhythms of considerable force. Unfortunately he has been almost forgotten in our art annals and the paintings of his last period, described by his wife as "small pictures of geometrical forms [on which] he would work for months making slight changes in colour and sometimes in form," have disappeared.[9]

Closely allied to Bruce was an even more obscure painter, Arthur Burdett Frost, Jr., son of the nineteenth-century American illustrator. Frost had gone to Paris in 1906, studied with Matisse the following year, and by 1913 was one of the group around Delaunay. He does not appear to have worked in a purely abstract manner until after his return to America about 1915 when, according to one account, he was converted by some of Bruce's work which that artist had sent him. But there is much confusion in the scanty information available on Frost and his pictures have all disappeared since his early death in 1918. He is mentioned here partly as an example of the little-known influence of Orphism on our early modernists, partly because those who knew his work thought highly of his abilities.[10]

The Orphic-Synchromist influence was not limited entirely to direct followers, but seeped into other American abstract work. It may be seen in the small brightly colored planes with which Arthur B. Davies tried for a time to clothe his idyllic nudes, while Delaunay's Tour Eiffel style is reflected, one suspects, in the dynamic movement of semi-abstract figure pieces by A. S. Baylinson and Frederick R. Shaler. Even Joseph Stella seems to have added some Orphic elements to his predominantly futurist style in the picture "Spring."

Such a mixture was entirely compatible, for futurism, while it was less concerned with precise color relations as space builders, was close kin to Orphism in its attempt to force dynamic three-dimensional motion into the static patterns of the cubists. For this purpose it invented a number of graphic symbols to indicate motion and speed in a given direction. Its most familiar device was the force line, sometimes curving sinuously but more often in the shape of repeated V's or rays like those of a searchlight. Its most characteristic paintings, which began to appear in Italy about 1911, were those which exalted the power and impersonal force of the machine, particularly the speeding automobile and airplane.

Traces of futurism had appeared in some work of the Synchromists (for example Macdonald-Wright's "Airplane Yellow and Orange"), but it had a more direct follower in the American Joseph Stella, who had been in contact with the Italian leaders of the movement during his travels abroad in 1909–1911. Soon after the Armory Show he painted his "Battle of Lights, Coney Island," a brilliant and explosive picture which translated the noise and glitter of his subject into modern pictorial terms. At almost precisely the same time Max Weber began a series of New York scenes, done between 1912 and 1916, which also applied futurist principles to the interpretation of the city's dynamism, as in his "Rush Hour, New York."

Stella and Weber followed, in general, the Italian founders of the movement, but the work of both shows many personal qualities. Stella's opulence and enthusiasm were reflected in the exuberance of his paintings, their complexity, glowing color, and glitter of many faceted planes. Weber's futurist pictures were also opulent, but in a more personal and sensuous manner; often he used a graceful curving line and fragments of human forms, as in his "Women and Tents" of 1913. While neither artist was to have many followers until the next decade, their futurist experiments were important, for they showed how abstract art could be infused with romantic feeling and applied, as we have shown in a previous chapter, to the interpretation of America's industrial civilization.

A related though more original art, owing something to futurism, something to Delaunay and the cubists, was being forged in Germany during the same years by the expatriate American artist Lyonel Feininger, who had partially abandoned his expressionist style about 1912. Feininger, too, used force lines and explosive arrangements of cubes to create dynamic and romantic values. But he did so with a delicate precision, balancing thrust against thrust, rigidly controlling both the motion and the emotion within the carefully wrought structure of his pictures. These prefigure in many ways, as Alfred Barr has pointed out, the work of Demuth and the American Immaculates,[11] but Feininger's work was little known in this country until after 1923 and it is doubtful that it had much influence on the formation of the style of the Immaculates.

Feininger was closely associated with the Blaue Reiter group in Munich but was not much affected by their work. Relatively few Americans were, although Albert Bloch did some decorative semi-abstractions in the manner of Franz Marc, and Konrad Cramer, German born, emulated Kandinsky's abstract expressionism after he came to the United States in 1911.

But it was Marsden Hartley who made the most personal use of German expressionism in an imposing group of roughly painted, free-form abstractions done between 1913 and 1915. Heavy and rhythmical, with richly modulated color, they are among the most original paintings of their kind by an American in these years. Neither flat, like cubist art, nor truly three-dimensional like the work of the futurists and the Synchromists, they establish a shallow depth in which the overlapping forms and the slight foreshortenings set up dynamic tensions of great force. They are also original in their use of recognizable symbols, such as the maltese cross which appears in several of the pictures done in Germany. These establish the "subject" of the painting without sacrificing its abstract character; they are there for a romantic purpose which is perhaps more important than their formal function in the design.

Strangely similar in many respects are the early abstractions of another very individual painter, Arthur G. Dove. Through quite different channels (he had no direct contact with German art) Dove developed a romantic style which was organized in the same shallow three-dimensional space as Hartley's and set up the same interlocking tensions. His occasional use of symbols in otherwise abstract compositions, such as "Nature Symbolized" or "Pagan Philosophy," was also akin to Hartley's and even more romantic in feeling. These are not entirely typical, however, for much of Dove's work was inspired by his strong devotion to nature and in general he preferred to work semi-abstractly, maintaining a larger quota of recognizable elements.

Still another painter may be grouped with Hartley and Dove for his dynamic, free-form abstractions in shallow space. This was John R. Covert, who had studied in Munich and Paris and had known Duchamp in New York during the first years of the war. His early career is obscure, but about 1919 he produced a series of collages which are both inventive and unusual. Using slightly three-dimensional objects such as string, dowel pins, and upholstery tacks, he wove them in and out in rhythmic patterns which give the illusion of overlapping or passing behind the painted forms of his pictures. Since he often covered these objects with paint, it seems clear that he was less interested in surface texture (like the cubists) or in incongruous combinations (like the Dadaists) than he was in creating spatial tensions which pull against the picture plane. Both he and Hartley painted pictures called "Brass Band" and in other works treated musical themes. Unfortunately, Covert gave up painting about 1923, apparently for financial reasons.

The dynamism, if that is not too strong a word, of Hartley, Dove, and Covert was reserved and primarily formal in character. To some extent it was an expression of romantic feeling for their subjects but this, except perhaps in Dove's case, seems of secondary importance. With John Marin, subject and form are interwoven to such a degree that one cannot successfully be weighed against the other. There can be no doubt that Marin's emotional, half-mystical feeling for New York played a large part in the formation, about 1915, of his unique brand of semi-abstract expressionism. To this extent he belongs with Stella, Weber, and the other early modernists who sought the spirit of the city. One is also tempted to compare his treatment of the Woolworth Building in 1912 with Delaunay's earlier pictures of the Eiffel Tower, although Marin apparently did not know these. But stylistically there is little similarity between Marin and any of his contemporaries. The streamlined forms of futurism obviously did not appeal to him. The explosive intensity of his vision was closer to Delaunay's, but it was embodied in harsh, angular, bent distortions quite different from the latter's cubes. Doubtless his style owed something to cubism and to the architectonic planes of Cézanne, both of which he had recently encountered in exhibitions at 291. Already, however, Marin was beginning to invent those personal, semi-abstract symbols which were to become so characteristic of his art. Already, too, he had proved his ability to organize them in abrupt, staccato patterns of great originality.

**54**

After the varied innovations of our painters in the period before 1920, abstract sculpture in America seems scanty and weak. Alexander Archipenko made important contributions in this field as early as 1911, but we can scarcely claim him since he did not settle here until many years later. Max Weber did a few pieces about 1915 which are perhaps the first totally abstract works by an American; these were only incidental to his painting, however. Our most advanced sculpture in this period was at the most semi-abstract, often quite representational, but even then making use of extremely simplified forms which derive, in part at least, from the abstract movement. It followed two general trends, one decorative, the other more monumental.

"Decorative" is perhaps misleading, for it suggests the thinly ornamental whereas we are dealing here with an art of almost classical contours and of flowing, sinuous lines. There was in it, at times, a rather mannered elegance betrayed in the exaggerated taper of a leg or other excesses of grace, but at its best it was vigorous and strongly built work. Its leading exponents were Elie Nadelman and Gaston Lachaise, whose sculpture shared closely the qualities above, though different in other respects. About 1907 Nadelman had experimented with cubic simplifications of the human form but soon gave these up for the full, rounded volumes which he combined in strangely exotic proportions throughout his career. Lachaise was both less subtle and more robust, his full-bodied nudes frankly sensual in a way that Nadelman's never were. Yet both might well have signed that part of the latter's explanatory letter to Stieglitz in which he said, "I employ no other line than the curve. . . The subject of any work of art is for me nothing but a pretext for creating significant form," [12] although one suspects Lachaise would have qualified the sentiment to give Eros his due.

From about 1913 on, another American, Paul Manship, developed a somewhat similar style which was more immediately popular since it was more obviously decorative. His rather archaistic simplifications of form seem now more superficial than those of Nadelman and Lachaise, but being more easily understood they may have helped to prepare the way for the more extreme modernists.

**55**

What we have called the monumental style was also developed chiefly by two men whose works shows certain similarities. Robert Laurent was the earlier. After a brief period of rather fantastic expressionist work he began, about 1916, to carve those monumental and massive figure compositions which are characteristic of his mature style. In 1917 William Zorach, who had been painting both Fauve and cubist pictures, turned to sculpture as his principal medium. While he carried some of the formal lessons he had learned from cubism into his carving, he, like Laurent, worked consistently in a representational vein with emphasis on strong formal organization. The art of both men in its large simplicity, its respect for the material in which they worked, and its faith (later modified) in direct carving is related to the modern classicism of Maillol and Despiau, though it also absorbed native elements from our folk art tradition. It was soon to become the dominant influence on a new generation of American sculptors.

As the first wave of abstract art receded about 1920, it seemed to some who had pinned their hopes on its future that American artists had failed, at least in part, to understand its true significance. "One cannot write of 'actual Cubism' in America, but only of the effort," said Andrew Dasburg who had himself been an abstract painter in the Synchromist line. "We lack the intellectual integrity to work logically within the limitations inherent in an idea. We want instead to gather what is best from many sources. . . This idea of combining a variety of forms of perfection into one complete ideal realization prevents any creative work being done which possesses the contagious force of Cubism. . . Though we fail in this . . . there are, among American artists, men of unusual talent whose work compares favorably with the best being done in Europe, excepting that of a few great figures." [13]

This perceptive appraisal puts its finger on several truths: that cubism demanded too intellectual a discipline for us, that the American artist tended to be eclectic and finally that, in spite of this, we produced abstract work of quality. But Dasburg failed to recognize (understandably in 1923) that our good work was more than the random product of "unusual talent," that it had, with all its diversity, some homogeneous character; that it established, in short, a system of abstract art which was more than the sum of its eclectic gleanings and as legitimate in its own way as the more rigid system of the cubists.

The central characteristic of our first abstract movement was its romantic dynamism, a quality which we had found in futurism, in Orphism, and to a lesser degree in German expressionism, but which we reinterpreted for our own purposes. These interpretations varied from the relatively orthodox ones of Stella, Bruce, and the Synchromists to others which were quite unlike anything being done abroad, particularly those of Hartley, Dove, and Marin. Somewhere between lay the work of Weber, Feininger, and several others. In spite of their personal differences, all of these men sought in abstraction a dynamic structure and a romantic spirit — which was perhaps the only way in which abstract art could be linked to our long romantic tradition. It is, indeed, the romantic half of the equation which seems the deeper; the dynamism was more variable and appears more often as a superficial overlay of modernity, particularly in the work of our minor artists. But the fact that so many of our best men found in this combination the means to a new expression of their American background as well as their personal feelings was proof that our traditions had not petrified beyond the possibility of growth.

It is difficult to draw a precise line between the first and second waves of abstract art in America, for certain of the earlier men — notably Marin, Dove, Stella, and Feininger — continued to work in this vein during the decade of the 1920's. But it is significant that all of these painted semi-abstractly and that several, like Feininger and Dove, showed at this time a tendency to return increasingly to nature. Of the other pioneers, Schamberg, Frost, and Shaler were dead, while Weber, McFee, Dasburg, Covert, Macdonald-Wright, Baylinson, Davies, and Zorach had given up abstraction by 1920 or shortly thereafter. At about the same time others like Sheeler and O'Keeffe moved toward semi-abstraction from their more extreme styles.

The leap from representational to abstract art may have been, after all, too big a one for most American artists to take at a single bound, for it involved a painful isolation not only from public acceptance, but from the country's artistic matrix — a source of support for all but the strongest. When the revolutionary fervor subsided a partial retreat followed in which the gains were consolidated and, to change the metaphor, woven more securely into the fabric of our traditions. This was the most significant development in our abstract art during the 1920's, although a lesser surge of experiment also took place in the same decade.

The group of artists who fashioned the principal compromise between abstract principles and American realism are sometimes called the precisionists, sometimes the Immaculates. Both words are descriptive of their smooth, precise technique and their compositions of sharp-edged, simplified forms painted in large areas of unmodulated color. As we have said in our discussion of the machine, they found in the mechanical and industrial forms of our civilization a theme which was naturally adapted to abstract treatment and which was also representative of modern America. It seems clear, however, that the formal appeal of their subject was uppermost, for they painted it with none of the romantic dynamism of the futurists, nor with any trace (one artist excepted) of Dada wit. They felt that a close affinity existed between mechanical functionalism and abstract art. In modern painting and sculpture, said William Zorach, the "interplay of form must function, it must correlate its parts into a whole in the same sense that a fine machine is . . . good or bad according to the perfection of the working relation of its parts." [14] To what extent this formal interest in the machine became an emotional feeling for its awesome precision is difficult to gauge.

The beginnings of the movement are to be found in the earlier period of our abstract art, but we have postponed considering them because of their close relation to its later development. About 1916 Morton L. Schamberg, who had experimented briefly with cubism and with abstract expressionism, started painting a series of machine pictures which, in spite of the apparent influence of Duchamp and

Picabia, have a serious and precise elegance far from the spirit of Dada. His machines were sometimes three-dimensional and closely related to actual models; often they were translated into flat patterns of soft blues, greens, yellows, and grays on a bare canvas. Four or five years later Charles Demuth evolved from the same sources a style which was to have a much greater effect on the Immaculates than Schamberg's. Demuth also had been influenced by cubism and he told Forbes Watson in 1923 that Duchamp had been "his strongest influence of late years." But these contacts can account for only a small part of the American artist's individual vision. His "Paquebot, Paris," painted in 1921, may be said to have created, in its essentials, the Immaculate style. Its use of machine forms, its delicate precision, its mixture of realism with abstract design were all to become the guiding principles of the new movement. Only the ray lines, which Demuth appropriated from futurism to enliven his compositions, were not taken over by those who followed him. Demuth, too, was one of the first to discover the aesthetic possibilities in the American industrial scene, which he began to paint in the early twenties. While his pictures of factories and grain elevators foreshadowed the interest of the Immaculates, they are again apart from the main line of development in their playful dynamism and their witty, Duchamp-like titles; only Demuth, of the Americans, would call a smokestack and a water tower "Aucassin and Nicolette" or see in a cluster of factory chimneys an "End of the Parade."

No one man was responsible for establishing the Immaculate vision; it seems rather to have been the result of a spontaneous development in the same direction and at the same time by several artists of whom Preston Dickinson, Charles Sheeler, and Georgia O'Keeffe were perhaps the most important. All of these had worked in an abstract or semi-abstract manner in the period 1914–1918; all turned about 1920 to a realism still strongly modified by abstract design. About 1918 Dickinson had painted "The Factory," but his work at this time showed a strong influence of Cézanne in its glitter of faceted planes, and while he came closer to the more sober style of the Immaculates in later pictures, such as "Industry," he never entirely gave up a kind

**59**

of lively surface enrichment. O'Keeffe is also a little apart from the main movement, not for technical or stylistic reasons, but because of the very personal and feminine character of her art. In her subtle shading, her bright, pure color, and her precise edges she is typically Immaculate, but she has never shown an interest in machine or industrial forms. Instead she has preferred to trace the sinuous curves of flowers, bleached bones on the desert, and other natural objects in which she has discovered a wealth of feminine symbolism.

Of the three it is Charles Sheeler who has been, from the beginning, the leading figure of the movement, although his art has never stood still at one purely Immaculate point. On the contrary, it has flowed with a kind of glacial deliberation from the semi-abstract work of 1914–1919 to an extreme realism in the 1930's and back toward semi-abstraction in the 1940's. Nevertheless Sheeler's painting during the decade of the 1920's may be said to have established the limits of the Immaculate style and to have explored most of the possible variations between these. At the abstract extreme is his "Church Street El," done in 1922. Here a New York scene is translated into a nearly geometrical pattern by a severe simplification of planes and volumes. But it is characteristic of both Sheeler and the Immaculates that, aside from these simplifications, the picture's abstract quality was established by the essentially naturalistic device of viewing the scene from a bird's-eye angle which emphasized, through its odd perspective, the rectangular design without doing overt violence to its "realism." At the other or realist extreme is Sheeler's "Upper Deck" of 1929, a picture which appears at first to be an almost photographic rendering of stays and ventilators. But the abstract qualities, though less obvious, are still predominant and may be sensed in the repetition, with variations, of the crisply generalized forms. In this painting, however, Sheeler has come a long way from his earlier work and even further from Demuth's "Paquebot, Paris," in which the ventilators are not only more abstract but have an almost anthropomorphic jauntiness compared with the sobriety of those in "Upper Deck." This was about as far towards realism as the Immaculate style could go without losing its preponderantly abstract character.

In the early 1920's Sheeler was joined by a number of artists who helped to develop the Immaculate style. One of the most consistent and serious of these was Niles Spencer who, with more somber color and a slightly freer technique, introduced a quiet romanticism into the movement without essentially altering its character. Other pioneers were George C. Ault, Stefan Hirsch, and Louis Lozowick, who were followed later in the decade by Gardner Hale, Jo Cantine, Elsie Driggs, Ralston Crawford, Peter Blume, and a good many more younger painters. In the early 1930's Francis Criss, with his deep perspectives of empty city streets, added another romantic note, faintly reminiscent of di Chirico, to the movement.

Even our best sculpture of this period, which continued to be that of Lachaise, Nadelman, Laurent, and Zorach, bears a certain relation to the work of the Immaculates. It was not a part of the movement, but it showed somewhat the same preoccupation with translating natural forms into basically abstract compositions. It was still our most advanced sculpture, the great body of work in this medium being, as Horace Brodzky said in 1921, "an awful concoction of suavity and caressable confectionery." He added, "I do not believe that five genuine sculptors exist in the United States," [15] and indeed it was not until the next decade that many new recruits of interest appeared in this field.

While the Immaculate movement was a compromise between realism and abstraction, it answered a deeply felt need and released much creative energy. Like most new movements, however, it also attracted those who codified its superficial traits into formulas requiring less creative effort. Rockwell Kent, for instance, had evolved several years before Sheeler a quite individual version of Immaculate art in illustrations which wedded sharp contours and simple volumes to the mannerism of William Blake; these were endlessly repeated by a host of minor illustrators (and to some extent by Kent himself) until they became very nearly as wooden as the blocks on which they were engraved. Similarly, at the end of the movement, Grant Wood fashioned a superficially Immaculate style which reduced villages to toy houses

**61**

and trees to wads of green cotton in a self-consciously primitive manner.

The Immaculate movement has never entirely died out. Painters like Niles Spencer and Francis Criss have worked consistently within its boundaries, and Sheeler in recent years has returned to it. But its heyday was in the 1920's and its most vital manifestations since then are to be found in the influence it has exerted on later and quite different phases of American art, especially on several of our realists and surrealists. If, in its pure form, it seems now a little cold and limited in its range of expression, it was for all that one of our most spontaneous and fertile modern movements and one which may claim to have been the first to acclimatize abstraction in America.

The Immaculates were not the only abstract artists of the 1920's. In the same decade the romantic dynamism of the previous decade expanded greatly and came nearer to establishing a unified movement than it had in the earlier period. While Marin and Dove continued to develop their individual styles, it was not their art but the more obvious and superficial dynamism of the futurists which became, apart from Immaculate work, the predominant abstract mode.

A number of influences, both native and foreign, contributed to the momentary victory of futurism over our other abstract styles. The sensitive use of futurist elements by Demuth in the early part of the decade and by Feininger, whose work began to be shown here in 1923, may have had some influence, but it was doubtless the more dramatic example of Joseph Stella which had the greatest effect. Stella had been a futurist since 1913, but his first one-man exhibition (at the Bourgeois Gallery) was not held until 1920. Even more important was the stir of admiration caused by his huge futurist panorama of the city, "New York Interpreted," which the Société Anonyme showed in 1922. Radiating from its central picture, "The Prow," the city's manifold aspects unfolded with a dynamic splendor which won for Stella a leading position in the new movement.

In the same years European futurism, which had been absent from the Armory Show, began to appear in America. The English futurist,

C. R. W. Nevinson, exhibited his paintings at Keppel's in 1919 and while he was here did a series of New York scenes which were shown at the Bourgeois Gallery the following year. These were inevitably compared with Stella's to the general disadvantage of the Englishman. In 1922 David Burliuk, hailed as the father of Russian futurism, settled in America and was soon widely publicized for his one earring and 125 flowered vests. In 1926 he printed a manifesto to accompany his picture in the Independents' Exhibition in which he proclaimed the "Radio Style," a new American brand of futurism. The following year his "Advent of the Mechanical Man" was the occasion for another manifesto on the Radio Style, "invented by David Burliuk," [16] but shortly thereafter he abandoned it. Finally, in 1926, the Italian futurists, who had founded the movement, at last had a New York exhibition.

Under these varied impulses and perhaps, too, because its spirit accorded well with the bustling optimism of the boom years before the depression, futurism became an almost fashionable expression of modernity. Robert Edmond Jones designed futurist stage sets for *Macbeth* which were called "the most extraordinary of their kind by an American." [17] Paul Burlin experimented with it briefly in such pictures as "Forces in Motion." Charles H. Walther modified his earlier cubist style in the new direction and painted typically futurist subjects like "Mechanism and Mechanist." John Storrs adapted it to sculpture by means of a rather superficial streamlining. And in every Independents Exhibition a host of younger artists, such as Theodore G. Haupt, Joseph Lomoff, T. K. Gado, and Torajiro Watanabe, interpreted New York in wildly swirling semi-abstract patterns.

Except for the work of Joseph Stella, the futurist movement of the 1920's seems today one of our thinnest accomplishments in the abstract field. Perhaps Leo Stein was right when he argued in 1925 that it was rooted in an essential fallacy: that this was a machine age which should be reflected in a machine art — whereas, said Stein, it is the least machinelike of all ages, in which the perfection of our modern inventions is as nothing compared with the imperfections of all our social machinery.[18] Nevertheless, the movement cannot be ignored, for it was the expression of serious convictions then widely held.

While futurism and Immaculate art accounted for the two main

**63**

streams of abstraction in the 1920's, there were also a number of individuals who explored other modes of abstract painting. Marin and Dove were perfecting their mature styles, which will be discussed at greater length in the next chapter; both had discovered during the twenties the most direct and economical means of expressing their deep love of certain aspects of America. In Marin's case, his personal shorthand had been simplified and disciplined until it could evoke with a few strokes the spirit of the Maine coast or the mountains of the southwest. Dove, in the same decade, experimented more widely, but perhaps his most successful work was a series of collages, such as "Grandmother" and "Goin' a-Fishin'," inspired more by native Yankee humor than by his recollections of cubist work in the same vein. In Philadelphia Arthur B. Carles developed a forceful abstract expressionism; Synchromism found a belated echo in the work of Alexander P. Couard; variations of cubism were produced by Paul Gaulois, Charles Logasa, and others.

But the most important new figure in the abstract field in these years was Stuart Davis. After the Armory Show Davis had gone through an expressionist phase strongly influenced by Van Gogh, but about 1920 he began to develop an entirely different abstract style which eventually mixed influences from Picasso, Léger, and other French modernists with the bright precision of the Immaculates and a very personal vision. His first painted imitations of cubist collages showed his skill in organizing flat patterns, a skill which was greatly enhanced in his later, severely architectonic compositions based on the forms of an egg beater. But Davis's most personal contribution was made in another series of semi-abstract canvases which revealed his flashes of humor and his sensitive feeling for the character and mood of a place or a subject. These revelations come with a kind of startling abruptness in staccato patterns which mix symbolic fragments of reality with abstract forms and are often punctuated by exuberant eruptions of scribbled line. In a way, Davis's art summarizes the best qualities of American abstraction in the 1920's, for it disciplined the futurists' dynamism and intensified the Immaculates' feeling for the object without their sacrifice of abstract force.

64

# 6

## REVOLUTION IN FORM

### abstract art today

The lean years which followed the economic depression of 1929 signaled the end of our second wave of abstract art. "In 1934 I became socially conscious as everyone else was doing in those days and became mixed up with the Artists' Congress," Stuart Davis told James Johnson Sweeney. Davis continued to work abstractly, although he added, "Lots of work was done, but little painting." [1] Many artists, however, felt the need of relating their art more closely to specific realities whether social or not. Burliuk abandoned his Radio Style and filled his "Day and Night" of 1930 with references to poverty and unemployment. Sheeler, Lozowick, and other Immaculates moved towards a greater naturalism. It was the decade of social realism and the painters of the American scene.

This condition lasted through the 1930's, although portents of the third abstract wave began to appear almost as soon as the second subsided and by the middle thirties had begun to assume the proportions of a new movement. One of the most significant circumstances was the closing by the Nazis of the Bauhaus School at Dessau and the subsequent emigration to the United States of many of its most famous teachers. Between 1930 and 1938 Werner Drewes, Josef Albers, Lyonel Feininger, Moholy-Nagy, and Herbert Bayer had arrived here in the order given; all were abstract painters and all except Feininger continued to teach in this country. Their numbers were swelled by the outbreak of the war in 1939 which brought William Stanley Hayter, Amédée Ozenfant, Piet Mondrian, Fernand Léger, and several other leading European modernists to America for varying periods.

At the same time many American artists, including some who were not themselves abstractionists, became alarmed at the chauvinistic extremes of the American-scene painters and the noisy propaganda of social realism as these movements were exploited by numberless minor followers. A humorous saint told Benjamin Kopman in 1935 never to "yield an inch to those art reformers who are steering the American scene into a dry land and . . . are slowly eating the flesh off American art, so that very soon we shall see Mr. Craven in full dress and high hat walking down the avenue with a skeleton on his arm"; it still seemed to Macdonald-Wright ten years later that "particularly in this country, many artists have retreated to the safe refuge of patriotism and the purportedly virile caricaturing of our under privileged people and places." [2]

These forces of discontent with social realism and reawakened interest in abstract art came to a focus in 1937 when a group of American artists who had begun again what G. L. K. Morris called "the quest for an abstract tradition," founded the society known as American Abstract Artists for the exhibition of their work and the general promotion of abstract art. Morris' statement in the catalogue of their second exhibition left no doubt that they were revolting in part against surrealism with "its bankrupt plastic language," but chiefly against traditional forms, of which he wrote, "the exploitation of American local color is the most oppressive at the moment." The contentious spirit of the group was underlined by their indiscriminate attack in a pamphlet in 1940, on virtually every art critic writing.

In 1935 the Whitney Museum had held an exhibition of Abstract Art in America which included several new names, such as those of Byron Browne, John Graham, Balcomb Greene, Karl Knaths, I. Rice Pereira, and Louis Schanker, most of them unknown in the abstract field before 1930 but destined to become prominent in the new movement. When the American Abstract Artists held their first show two years later thirty-nine exhibitors were represented and the number grew steadily in succeeding exhibitions. From about 1940, or perhaps a little earlier, the new interest in abstract painting began to be reflected in its growing representation on Fifty-seventh Street and in

the large museum annuals; after the war it took over one of these completely.[3] Representational painters like Minna Citron and Arnold
Blanch became abstractionists overnight and others like Ralston Crawford, Fletcher Martin, or the sculptor, Robert Laurent, began to introduce more abstract qualities into their work without so radically
changing direction. For the first time in its history the Art Students
League permitted abstract art to be taught in its classes, and thousands
of younger artists embarked on the abstract experiment. "The naturalistic art of our time is unredeemable," wrote Clement Greenberg, "as
it requires only taste to discover; and the sheer multitude of those who
still practice it does not make it any more valid." [4]

But the most persuasive argument for abstract art in recent years
has been that art itself. While many of our traditional forms of painting have shown extraordinary elasticity and creative force, abstraction
has been the most powerful stimulus to the artistic imagination in the
1940's; for the first time in our history it has overshadowed the other
modern movements and has probably produced a larger and more
varied body of creative work than any one of the latter, though not,
perhaps, than their combined sum. We shall try to separate the strands
of the movement less for chronological order than in accordance with
the kinds of art produced and the relation of these to our earlier abstract traditions.

Of the two main streams of international abstraction, the purely
classical and rational one had started in this country as a bare trickle
with a few cubist pictures by Weber, McFee, Walther, Zorach, and
some others. In the 1920's the chief exponents of this tradition had
been the Immaculates. They were not, of course, the strict geometri-
cians that the cubists and the various European constructivists were,
but their art was built on an underlying geometrical framework and it
had the clarity, the serenity, and the ordered beauty of the classical
vision.

In our third abstract period this kind of painting has been in the
minority, but it has been far from negligible and more varied in its
forms than hitherto. One strand has renewed or grown out of the Immaculate style. Niles Spencer has continued to work in this manner

**67**

and Sheeler has returned to it in such recent pictures as "Incantation," which is more abstract in its organization than anything he has done since the early 1920's. Another Immaculate, Ralston Crawford, has transformed it into a more completely abstract style while retaining its characteristic precision and something of its feeling for the object.

But it is typical of all our abstract art in recent years that it has drawn less on our scattered native tradition than it has on the more compact European movements. Thus the various phases of cubism have been reëxamined by such painters as A. E. Gallatin, G. L. K. Morris, and Bradley Walker Tomlin; constructivism has had its influence on Harry Bertoia, Charles G. Shaw, Balcomb Greene, and I. Rice Pereira; the Dutch *De Stijl* movement on Fritz Glarner. Of these, Pereira has worked most consistently within the strict intellectual discipline which marks this kind of art at its purest; she has also enlarged its technical boundaries with her brilliant experiments in painting on several superimposed transparent planes of glass or plastics. In comparison, the lyrical note of Tomlin and the mysterious forms of Greene seem nearly romantic, but they have their own quite different intellectual force.

It is in our modern architecture, however, that the classical spirit has manifested itself most widely. The preëminently orderly and rational character of the International Style, as it was developed in Europe by Le Corbusier, Oud, Gropius, Mies van der Rohe, and others, has had a growing influence on American building since early in the 1930's. Perhaps one reason that it has transplanted so well is that its precise and simple forms were in close accord with the same native spirit that produced the Immaculates; if Le Corbusier's houses were "machines for living," their pictures, as someone has remarked, were "machines to live with." Moreover, the functional aspects of the International Style have accorded well with our popular admiration of science and engineering, our widespread delight in speed and efficiency, and our complacent belief in the virtues and rewards of an industrial civilization. It is true that one of our leading architects, Frank Lloyd Wright, has generally shown a preference for more romantic forms, but even Wright has at times worked parallel to the International

Style, and our other modern architects have used it consistently and well, at least in their large public buildings.

It is difficult to draw a line between purely classical abstraction and that which is closely related but modified by a dynamism with romantic overtones. Much of our earlier abstract art, especially the futurist pictures of Weber and Stella and the quite different work of Feininger and Stuart Davis, was of this latter kind. Unlike the dynamism of Marin, Dove, and Hartley, theirs was wedded to the clarity and precision of classical forms; at times it even partook of cubism's geometry. Of the four, only Feininger and Davis have continued to develop in this direction in recent years. But while both have been given retrospective exhibitions by the Museum of Modern Art and have established well-deserved reputations in their field, their direct influence on younger painters has been relatively small. In Feininger's case, particularly, his extraordinary embodiment of romantic vistas within a crystalline structure has been too personal and difficult an equilibrium for others to attempt.

Most modern art in this dynamic-classical vein is related either to conventional futurism or, in a very general way, to the style of Davis. The futurist influence has diminished steadily since its flowering in the early 1920's, but it did produce about 1935 a number of strong canvases by Abraham Rattner, and it has also found expression in the work of Robert Jay Wolff and Johannes Molzahn.

In what we may call the Davis line, though entirely personal, is one phase of the work of Karl Knaths, who has painted in a variety of styles, both representational and abstract. Even in the latter mode, Knaths has explored expressionism, the linear fantasy of Klee, and the static, classical order of cubism. But in a number of pictures he, like Davis, has enlivened cubist design with dynamic tensions; like Davis, too, he has made this combination serve him both in purely formal abstractions, such as his "Maritime" of 1930, and in semi-abstractions, such as his "Duck Flight" of 1948, the latter revealing, half symbolically, the same feeling for the Massachusetts coast that Davis established in his "Summer Landscape." These parallels are apparently accidental rather than the result of direct influence; they show that two artists who are genuinely moved by native themes could translate their study of Matisse, Picasso, Braque, Léger, and Miró into a peculiarly American art capable of expressing that emotion.

Something of the same native quality and the same formal means are to be found in the abstract sculpture of Alexander Calder. The ingenious construction of his mobiles and their plastic wit (particularly in those which exaggerate the essence of bird and animal forms) have often struck observers as a distillation of Yankee traits; the humor, though wryer and sharper, has also been compared with that of Davis. On the formal side, the precise architecture of Calder's flat cutouts and the obvious dynamism of sculpture that sways and moves in changing patterns is plain enough.

But already in Calder's work, or in that of a painter like Carl Holty, we see a tendency to escape from pure dynamic structure into a more fluid arrangement of free, organic, or amorphous shapes which owe their closest allegiance to the abstract surrealism of Arp, Miró, and Klee. This is both a less dynamic, less severely architectonic art and a more romantic one, in which undertones of surrealism's automatism and psychological introspection persist even though the total effect is quite different.

This kind of art, which balances delicately between classical and romantic forms, is rather rare, however. Many more of our painters have gone over wholeheartedly to romantic abstraction, often under a strong surrealist influence. One of the most sensitive of these was Arshile Gorky during the seven or eight years before his tragic death in 1948. Like other abstract surrealists, Gorky devised a private symbolism which one must read like a cryptogram, half baffled by the layers of hidden meaning but continuously rewarded by sudden insights into a personality which André Breton aptly called "wild and tender." [5] Gorky's style with its wandering line and its amorphous stains of color also approaches the unattainable "pure psychic automatism" which is part of the anti-aesthetic credo of surrealism. But, again like much other abstract surrealism, his art is not in reality antiaesthetic; rather it establishes a different kind of order based on a personal calligraphy and a fluid counterpoint of line and shape.

**70**

In endless personal variations this introspective art has become one
of the most widely practiced branches of abstraction today. A strong
compulsion, rooted perhaps in the insecurity of our times and a distrust of the powers of reason, has turned many artists from more objective forms of art to this intuitive probing of mind and being. Gorky
himself had abandoned abstract expressionism for his final style.
Tomlin has left a modified cubism to weave free forms with a sensitive
running line. Lawrence Kupferman has stopped painting realistic Victorian houses to flow bright colors into blurred, kaleidoscopic patterns.
The styles are as many and as different as the personalities of those
who produce them. They range from the sharp, quasi-geometrical
constructions of Charles Howard to the swirling network of lines and
spots of Jackson Pollock; from the Dada-like precision of Jimmy
Ernst to the jeweled viscera of Charles Seliger; from the fragile elegance of Mark Rothko (before his very recent change in style) to the
grotesque and brooding images of William Baziotes. They are the
plastic language, in equally personal guise, of Boris Margo, André
Racz, Gerome Kamrowski, Seymour Franks, Cady Wells, and a good
many other serious artists. They have been tortured by perhaps a thousand ardent students into as many meaningless scribbles, blots, and
joyously erotic symbols.

Work in this vein is more international in character than the abstractions, say, of Marin or Stuart Davis — not because it draws more
heavily on foreign sources but because it is chiefly concerned with the
physical and metaphysical essence of man rather than with his relation
to nature, society, or those other aspects of life which have distinctive
national color. Internationalism of this sort is not an aim in itself, nor
a question of style; it is only "the natural consequence," as Robert
Motherwell has put it, "of dealing with reality on a certain level." [6]
As in all movements, however, this one has not always existed in its
"pure" state; in other words, it has sometimes expressed emotions that
*are* rooted in our country or its life. Needless to say, this deviation is
not, of itself, either superior or inferior — only different.

An art of this kind was developed with relative independence by one
of our most original abstract painters, Arthur G. Dove. We have seen

**71**

that Dove, much earlier in the century, had evolved a rhythmical, dynamic, often symbolic style somewhat akin to that of Hartley, though less massively expressionist. During the 1930's Dove gradually loosened his forms from their semigeometrical boundaries. They became now flamelike organic patterns, now irregular splotches of color which built up calligraphic structures like enlarged Chinese characters. Yet in spite of their amorphous nature, Dove's pictures are nearly always related to specific aspects of the American scene which moved him: to the farm and the sea or the stately lines of an old flour mill. The difference between his art and that of the surrealists is great, but it is more a question of subject than means. One cannot even say that he dug less deeply into the subconscious mind than they, for his emotional response to nature was perhaps embedded as far below the level of consciousness as the libido of Gorky, and he used approximately the same formal means to express it. But he dug in a different place and exhumed a very different treasure.

To some extent there has been a fusion between Dove's organic abstractions from nature and those of the more international, surrealist-related group. James Thrall Soby has pointed out the community of feeling in the work of Dove and that of the young painter Theodoros Stamos whose irregular, archaic forms are as romantic an interpretation of nature as those of the older man, though more darkly somber with the introspection of our time. Adolph Gottlieb has stayed closer to surrealism in his use of the compartmented pictograph which stems from Klee and Torres-García, but his employment of native symbols rather than their more fantastic images relates him also to this group. It could even be extended to include aspects of the work of Rothko and Baziotes, for the dividing line is tenuous and depends more on shades of feeling than it does on formal differences.

This organic, intuitive style has also tended to join with still another kind of romantic abstraction which stems principally from the post-cubist work of Picasso. Even in his most romantic phases, Picasso retained an incisive line and an austere structure which are essentially opposed to automatism and the amorphous. Nevertheless a painter like Robert Motherwell has succeeded, rather remarkably, in harmonizing these conflicting characteristics; his art, as he has said, "consists of a dialectic between the conscious (straight lines, designed shapes, weighed color, abstract language) and the unconscious (soft lines, obscured shapes, *automatism*) resolved into a synthesis which differs as a whole from either." [7] In quite a different way, the recent work of Max Weber, since his return to abstraction in the 1940's, rests on somewhat the same resolution. He has felt, as almost every abstract artist has, the impact of Picasso's genius; he appears also to have been influenced by surrealists like Matta. But the exuberant linear structure which Weber builds and the counterpoint of looser color areas which he plays against it are his own and grow naturally out of his earlier style. Many of our younger artists, however, have been content to follow more directly the example of Picasso's later work. It is unmistakably reflected, though with personal variations, in the painting of John Graham, Byron Browne, Louis Krassner, and John Ferren.

Finally, we must consider abstract expressionism which, historically, was the earliest romantic form of abstract art and which has never entirely disappeared from our painting. It had flowered during our first period in the work of Hartley and Cramer, certain paintings of Weber, and especially those of Marin. In the 1920's it diminished in volume but was kept alive by the last and by a few other individuals such as Arthur B. Carles. In recent years, though still in the minority, it has again expanded, following in part Marin's native line, in part the earlier European tradition.

Marin's own work in these years is the purest, most forceful abstract expressionism we have yet produced. The explosive intensity of his emotion is most spontaneously embodied in a series of brilliant water-colors in which the slashing strokes, the sudden angular distortions, and the calculated tensions of arbitrary color tug against the flat surface of the paper and the boundary of the frame without ever destroying their autonomy. His feelings, like his forms, are disciplined, focused, and thereby intensified. "I can have things that clash," he wrote, "I can have a jolly good fight going on — there is always a fight going on where there are living things but — I must be able to control this fight at will with a — Blessed Equilibrium."

> *In the doing of all this* [he added]
>    *terms*
>
>       *abstract*
>       *concrete*
>       *third or fourth dimen-*
>       *sion*    *bah*    *dont*
>       *bother us* —[8]

Marin has always disliked the word "abstract" and maintained with some justice that it is the essence of his subject, the stoniness of rock, the structure and motion of the sea that he strives to capture. But to purify this inner reality and give it emotional significance he has developed a set of very personal, nearly abstract, symbols. In addition he has frequently compartmented his subjects with heavy lines or broken them into planes which owe something to Cézanne and the cubists. It is true, however, that of all our abstract painters none has mirrored a deeper love for the sharply native aspects of both our landscapes and our cities. In his person and his art Marin is richly and rewardingly American.

In the catalogue of the Marin exhibition at the Museum of Modern Art, Marsden Hartley wrote: "You will never see water colors like these of John Marin again so take a good look and remember, and if you are a painter, don't try to cope with the style because the style in this case is several times the man." Perhaps this explains why Marin has had few direct followers although he is admired by a great many younger painters and has affected their work in a general way.

A more easily traceable influence, though not on the whole a very large one, has been exerted by Central European expressionism, particularly the early style of Kandinsky, whose work became better known here in the 1930's than it had been before. This has been augmented by the example and the teaching of the German-born Hans Hofmann, who came to America in 1930. Among Hofmann's pupils, the young Jackson Pollock stands out for his impetuous use of the expressionist vocabulary in such pictures as "The She-Wolf," painted in 1943 before he turned to his linear, mazelike abstractions. The work of Paul

Burlin is in a somewhat similar vein, although generally more representational. Also in the European tradition are such painters as William de Kooning and John Von Wicht, while a more native kind of abstract expressionism, remotely related to the art of Marin in feeling, though more international in style, has been developed by Vaclav Vytlacil and by Karl Knaths in certain earlier pictures like "Turkey in the Straw" and in much of his recent work.

Our abstract sculpture, which has finally flowered abundantly in the years since 1930, has followed the same general directions as our painting, but its development has been complicated by certain technical problems which have had aesthetic consequences. One of these has been the long dominance of a faith in direct carving as the only true method of creating sculptural quality. As we have said before, this concept was born early in the century in reaction against the prevailing romantic naturalism of the Rodin tradition. It returned sculpture to the simple, monumental forms of primitive or classical art; it insisted that the nature of the material and the sculptor's technique must play an important part in the aesthetic effect, particularly that stone sculpture must look compact and stony, that it must show, at least in parts, the marks of the tools which hewed it, even that it must preserve, if possible, traces of the shape of the original boulder from which it was cut.

Zorach and Laurent, our earliest exponents of direct carving, have continued to use this method to create representational work with an underlying abstract structure, although both have moved in the direction of romantic realism and can more logically be considered under that heading. Since about 1930 they have been joined by John B. Flannagan, José de Creeft, Ahron Ben-Shmuel, Saul Baizerman, Chaim Gross, and a great many others who have worked in approximately the same vein. Several of these have markedly increased the abstract content of their work. De Creeft's massive, rhythmical figures are conceived as a textural counterpoint of rough and polished volumes bounded by an elastic, curving line. Gross has introduced an exuberant, baroque design into an art which is usually more static and classical.

**75**

Baizerman, though not a carver, has also wedded technique and material to aesthetic ends in his use of hammered copper to create a monumental art with romantic overtones in the sensitive blurring of the forms. More than any of the others, John B. Flannagan revealed the compressed archaic images which his eye found in the shapes of native field stone; "the purpose," he wrote, "is to approximate the abstract cubical elemental forms, and to preserve the identity of the original rock so that it seems hardly carved, rather to have endured so always — inevitable." [9]

It will be seen that there was nothing antipathetic to abstraction in the widely held belief that the sculptor must express the nature of his material and technique. Indeed the grain of polished wood or stone and the shine of metal have been used in complete abstractions by Warren Wheelock and in certain early ones by Isamu Noguchi to enhance the design without destroying its compact monumentality. The sense of the material had, however, a limiting effect on the kind of abstraction which could be produced. The direct carver was limited by the size and shape of his stone or log and by the convention which grew out of this and held that all sculpture must be solid, self-contained, and unmarred by fragile excrescences. The worker in metal could not paint it red or blue, could not hammer it beyond its ductile limits, could not even (logically) cast it in the resemblance of modeled clay.

While these beliefs are still widely held and still produce much vigorous contemporary sculpture, there has also been a strong reaction against them which has permitted sculpture to take part more fully in the abstract movement, particularly in the direction of free, organic, surrealist-related forms. To achieve these, however, it was necessary to bring sculpture closer to the aesthetics of painting, to focus it on the image rather than the material — a more difficult problem because of sculpture's sheer bulk. The sculptor, said Herbert Ferber, "contributes to the dilemma when he is seduced by the beauty of the object; when his surrender to the pleasure of the material, the contour of the line, imposes on him the esthetics of the artisan," for it is only "when the sculptor has achieved the transmutation of the material into an image in the immediate and intimate way proper to his own artistic personality

76

[that] the audience will see — a work of art. When he has done less he will have produced — an object." [10]

The freer abstract sculpture which has resulted from this revolt has followed, as in painting, two quite different paths, one classical, the other romantic. The classical branch has been the smaller but also the earlier, for it was introduced in America by the Russian-born sculptor, Alexander Archipenko, who settled here in 1923. Archipenko had pioneered in a kind of cubist abstraction based on the human form; he had also been the first to pierce his sculpture with voids which formed a part of the composition and to hollow out concavities in places normally convex, creating a reverse counterpoint on natural forms. For many years he was the most advanced sculptor in America and the influence of his innovations (as distinct from his personal style) has been great. The spatial aspects of his work have tended to unite with the influence of the European constructivists, particularly the light and airy structures of metal, plastics, and wire done by the Russians Gabo and Pevsner. These have been closely paralleled here in the open, geometrical forms of Ibram Lassaw, Richard Lippold, Isamu Noguchi, Theodore J. Roszak, and others, at least at certain stages of their development. Machine forms have also played a part in this kind of sculpture. Work in the Dymaxion factory first interested Emma Lu Davis in abstract shapes and Noguchi, too, has paid his respects to the machine in his "Abstraction (Windmill)" and similar pieces.

Yet all of these sculptors (with the exception, so far, of Lippold) have felt a compulsion towards a more romantic kind of abstraction expressed in more fluid organic shapes. Here the influence of Arp, Lipchitz, and lately Henry Moore has been predominant. As in the painting of Motherwell, many hybrid pieces have been created which play the classical forms against the romantic ones. Noguchi mixes biology and mechanics in his "1000 h.p. Heart" or suspends a strange "Lunar Infant" in a precise magnesite frame. Lassaw cages his weird "Uranogeod" in his geometrical steel rectangles.

Far more frequently, however, our abstract sculptors have broken decisively with constructivist aims and devised their own purely romantic forms. The rational serenity of a classical art has been hard to

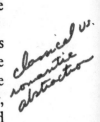

maintain; "the world is fundamentally and seriously disquieted," said Roszak in explanation of his own change of style, "and it is difficult to remain unmoved and complacent in its midst." [11] In response, his sculpture has moved from "Spatial Constructions" and "Pierced Circles" to some of the most wildly biomorphic images of "Anguish" or "Surge" which our times have produced. Something of the same nightmare quality exists in the work of David Smith, Seymour Lipton, Peter Grippe, Herbert Ferber, and David Hare. While Smith has wrought more objective symbols of modern life, the group as a whole has preferred to work with the subjective images of surrealism's dark foreboding.

Although these men have denied the spirit of constructivism, they have continued to owe much to its method, and this is also true of several other sculptors who have used its light open forms to create a more poetic romanticism than that of the surrealist-related group. Both Noguchi, in his big slablike constructions, and Calder, in his mobiles and stabiles, have retained, in spite of their organic shapes, a precise balance and a calligraphic elegance which is not so far removed from classicism as might at first appear. On a somewhat different level Leo Amino and Mary Callery have translated constructivism into an art of gay or gentle rhythms.

Finally, there has been a smaller branch of romantic abstract sculpture which has worked with the equally fluid but more compact forms of Brancusi and Arp, though not necessarily under their influence. One of our most individual artists in this line is Hugo Robus, whose boneless and slightly erotic figures flower with a kind of *art nouveau* vivacity which is stronger than it looks. C. Ludwig Brummé and Mitzi Solomon have also translated human structure into terms of more primitive organic growth while on the purely abstract side José de Rivera, Emma Lu Davis, Noguchi, and a good many others have made their personal variations on the amoebic shapes of Arp or the Brancusi egg. From their experiments and those of painters in the same vein, this kind of art has spread to modern furniture, advertisements, store windows, and other branches of industrial design where its more superficial decorative possibilities have been fully exploited.

**78**

Looking back at the last ten or fifteen years, it seems plain that our abstract art has been more varied and vigorous in this period than in either of its earlier manifestations. The classical branch, though still the smaller, has far outgrown the conservative vision of the Immaculates and has reëxplored the methods of cubism and constructivism. The romantic branch has expanded beyond the various kinds of expressionism and futurism, which earlier accounted for this part of the movement, and has found in the free form, surrealist-related trend a new kind of romantic vocabulary. This will probably emerge as the dominant abstract vein of the last decade, for it has not only flourished in a great number of "pure" guises but has also blended at many points with other kinds of abstraction, both romantic and classical.

# 7

## THE TRADITION

### impressionism and romantic realism

The impact of abstraction and expressionism, of the machine and surrealism created a new art in America and profoundly altered the older forms. But it did not destroy them. Some, like pure impressionism, lost vitality and became academic formulas; others, including various kinds of realism and romanticism, have continued to flourish with a freshness and strength that has sometimes fluctuated but has never been extinguished. Why this is so it is difficult to say, for the life of art forms is determined by complex forces which can be guessed but not measured. Two reasons, however, seem fairly clear: forms survived because they were rooted in the needs and beliefs of some part of our people and they survived in proportion to their ability to grow, either in their own way or, more often, by assimilating new life from the more revolutionary movements to which they were theoretically opposed. We have already seen how this operated in the case of the Immaculates, but there the assimilation was so great that their art became more closely related to abstraction than to native realism. In the movements which we shall now discuss the traditional forms, though constantly modified, remained dominant.

As the twentieth century opened, the most advanced style of the day was a darkly romantic one of slashing brushwork and broadly impressionistic effects. This should scarcely have seemed revolutionary in 1900, for it had been introduced in America by Frank Duveneck some twenty-five years earlier and had been increasingly popular with Munich school students and those of William Merritt Chase ever since. Nevertheless American critics were still divided as to its merits. Sada-

**80**

kichi Hartmann called it "the cult of sketchiness," and remarked that "if art continues in this weird fashion . . . it will soon be reduced to . . . a few lines and dots and some cross hatching." Frank Jewett Mather, Jr., referred to those "emphatic persons who, to judge by their works, paint in horrid orgasms." On the other hand, J. N. Laurvik called it "the beginning of a new movement in our art life," and Robert Henri defended it obliquely when he wrote that "what is necessary for art in America, as in any land, is first an appreciation of the great ideas native to the country and then the achievement of a masterly freedom in expressing them." [1]

Henri was the focal point of this dark impressionism in America. His own style, which had been formed partly by the native Duveneck-Sargent-Chase tradition, partly by his study of Manet, Hals, and Velásquez, made a brilliant if somewhat superficial use of the rapid, spontaneous stroke, the free drawing with the brush, and the *alla prima* technique. But it was as a teacher and a liberal leader of the Eight that his influence was greatest. His pupil, George Bellows, and his colleague in the Eight, George Luks, carried the style to its most forceful and extreme conclusions. In less extreme form it was also the style of John Sloan, Eugene Higgins, William Glackens, and Everett Shinn during the decade 1900–1910. It was closely associated, therefore, with that awakening interest in the human aspects of urban and industrial life which we have already discussed. As a formal means for expressing the essentially romantic spirit of the whole group it was admirably suitable. Within its rather flexible limits the humor, the pathos, the violence, the color, and even the gentle Stevensonian poetry of the city could be captured in pictorial terms which echoed the warmth and sentiment of the subject.

There was indeed much personal variety in its handling. Glackens' pearly grays and shimmering surfaces captured the idyllic aspects of childhood or the elegance of the city's shops and restaurants. Sloan and Luks were both more interested in dramatic episode and individual types; but while Luks saw his "Little Madonna" through a haze of sentiment which is expressed in the literal haze of the painting, Sloan's observations of the crowd around the "Hairdresser's Window" are more matter of fact, his handling direct and less romantic with a touch of good-natured satire in it. For pure athletic violence, both in subject and brushwork, none equaled George Bellows' early work of about 1909; there is indeed an almost demented frenzy in his "Both Members of This Club." In contrast to the gusto and optimism of these men, Eugene Higgins alone saw the dark side of the picture and turned the same free broad handling with a heavier touch to brooding images of poverty and labor.

Perhaps the greatest accomplishment of dark impressionism, how-ever, was in the field of drawings, prints, and illustration where it had its black-and-white equivalent in a sketchy style of deceptively casual line, sometimes combined with freely smudged shading or flicked-on high lights of Chinese white. Many of the leading painters in this move-ment had been trained as newspaper artists and continued to do some of their best work in occasional prints and illustrations. Sloan's etchings of New York and Glenn O. Coleman's drawings of its streets are perhaps the purest expression of their sharp and humorous observation, while the illustrations which the former, with Glackens and Shinn, did for the novels of Paul de Kock have great vivacity and wit. In this period American illustration flowered as it has not since. Luks, Bellows, Jerome Myers, May Wilson Preston, Henry Raleigh, the young Boardman Robinson, and Arthur G. Dove all contributed their lively comments on the drama of character and situation, while somewhat later the drawings and prints of George Overbury ("Pop") Hart continued the picaresque tradition.

But the renaissance had hardly begun before it was over. The style which had seemed so vital and even revolutionary in the first decade of the century, no longer looked so after the Armory Show of 1913. Several of the group, especially Glackens and Sloan, became interested in different problems and began to move away from romantic interpre-tation of the American scene. Others remained more faithful to their original aims and methods, but in doing so they may well have hastened the death of dark impressionism. Bellows and Luks, particularly, in attempting to force new vitality into it, pushed it to its limits and beyond, until it approached a caricature of vigor. Bellows seems to have realized that his fight pictures were an ultimate achievement in loose and slashing handling, for he returned in his later work to a quieter realism. But Luks, never willing to relinquish his revolutionary status, continued to the end to dash his paint on canvas in ever emptier pyrotechnics, although his final decline cannot erase the memorable images of "The Old Duchess," "The Spielers," "Hester Street," and those other early canvases into which he had poured such genuine humor and pathos.

The final extinction of dark impressionism cannot be blamed on any of these, however. Even before 1910 its vigorous brushwork was beginning to lose spontaneity and become an academic formula. Arnold Friedman has remarked that a common trick among young students "was to paint a head the best way one could and then with the paint still wet make quick, extra strokes with a large, dry brush over it, thus accomplishing the 'Sargent stroke.'"[2] Abandoned gradually by the more creative men, the style languished and passed finally into the academic repertoire of Charles Hawthorne, Wayman Adams, and from them to other younger academicians who still practice it today.

At the same time that dark impressionism was in its last flower, the "light" or more orthodox impressionist movement was also in its final creative stage. During the last fifteen years or so of the nineteenth century it had flourished in two independent lines: that of Winslow Homer, who had evolved his own vigorous plein-air style out of American realism; and that of Theodore Robinson, John H. Twachtman, Mary Cassatt, Childe Hassam, and J. Alden Weir, who were indebted in varying degrees to French impressionism with its pointillism and its sensuous poetry of light and color. Both kinds continued with much vigor in the opening decade of the twentieth century when Homer and Twachtman were still painting. But after 1910, with these two and Robinson dead, the twin lines began to coalesce and become conventionalized. Weir lived until 1919, Cassatt until 1926, and Hassam until 1935, but their best work, with few exceptions, was done before 1910.

After that date a few younger painters did indeed manage to breathe new life into impressionism, although their accomplishments now seem minor ones. Ernest Lawson's jewel-like color, Gifford Beal's blunt touch and holiday spirit, Carl Frieseke's tender, restrained, and often sentimental idyls, and even today the robust and spontaneous style of Waldo Peirce are evidence that the movement did not die easily. Its influence on others, who were not actually of it, has also been considerable. Literally hundreds of our landscape painters owe some debt to its technique and a greater one to its high color and its delight in the effects of sun and atmosphere, while Homer's influence has dominated American water-color painting until quite recent times.

In France the pure visual realism of impressionism had been modified from the beginning by painters like Cézanne and Renoir; it had then evolved towards other formal values in the art of the postimpressionists, Van Gogh, Seurat, Bonnard, and the rest. In America no evolution on such a scale took place and no real postimpressionist movement existed. Our development was telescoped by the impact of the Armory Show, and we leapt into abstraction from the shaky springboard of broken color. Nevertheless there were a few individual painters in America who attempted with some success the postimpressionist synthesis of plein-air brilliance and formal organization.

The earliest was Maurice Prendergast, who in the early 1890's had been working in a delicately impressionist style closer to Whistler than to Homer or Monet. Late in that decade he discovered Cézanne, probably the first American to appreciate the French artist's aims. In the first ten years of the new century Prendergast developed his own mature style, which borrowed surprisingly little from the master of Aix. Using the pointillism of the impressionists, which he enlarged into squarish patches of pure color, he wove his spots into patterns which sometimes receded sinuously into deep space but more often were arranged in a shallow perspective parallel to the picture plane. The innocent joyousness of his vision and his decorative flair have somewhat obscured the importance of his formal innovations, but Prendergast, as Lloyd Goodrich has pointed out, may well claim to be the first modernist among our painters.[8]

**84**

Only a little later than Prendergast and in some ways resembling him was Jerome Myers, who had started painting the lower East Side in the 1880's. About 1905 Myers began to lighten and organize his dark impressionism, and in the next ten years he developed a gently lyrical style of dancing surface patterns. At about the same time Allen Tucker, who had studied with Twachtman, found in Van Gogh (as William Glackens found in Renoir) the means to a personal transformation of impressionism, although the work of both men was a little overshadowed by unavoidable comparisons with their sources.

Oddly, from the point of view of time, one of the most complete and personal blends of impressionism and abstract design was made by Arnold Friedman in the ten or twelve years before his death in 1946. Friedman reversed the usual evolution, for he started as a painter with a strong sense of design, at one time influenced by Modigliani, and gradually added the impressionist elements of rough impasto and glowing broken color. With the latter he achieved a luminosity of peculiar depth and intensity. Demarcating lines disappeared and his massive compositions were so closely integrated with the glittering surface of his canvases that they are almost impossible to reproduce in black and white.

In spite of these creative manifestations, impressionism as a movement died early in the century. Its chief inheritors were again the academicians: first men of some sensitivity like Henry Ranger, Edward Redfield, and Elmer Schofield, then legions of formula painters who learned the trick of broken color and turned its bluish shadows into lurid purple ones, its high key into a monotonous glitter.

In the end it was the longer and more sober tradition of romantic realism which proved most durable. Though closely related in feeling to both kinds of impressionism, it was more flexible because it was not bound to technical preoccupations with either pointillism or slashing brushwork. From Allston in the opening years of the nineteenth century to the Hudson River School and the pre-Civil War genre painters, then on to Inness, Hunt, Martin, and so many others at the end of the century, it had taken a hundred guises without changing its essential character: that of realism slightly modified by various formal devices for more expressive and romantic effect. It is tempting to call it a cautious expressionism in which the distortions of natural forms were always subservient to the "real" image. This would be an accurate description of its outward appearance but not of its inner spirit, for it was based on a philosophy of art which held that only those distortions were justified which intensified truth, be it the character in a portrait, the shape and relation of things, or the moods which nature awakened in man.

Something of this philosophy was carried into the early twentieth century by the group called "The Tonal School of America" — men like Henry W. Ranger, J. Francis Murphy, Dwight Tryon, Henry Golden Dearth, and a great many other belated followers of the Barbizon School who still painted in its soft, misty, and intimate manner. This was one of the most popular and widespread kinds of romantic realism about 1900, but already it was beginning to run thin for the Barbizon influence had started in America half a century before and even Ranger's infusions of impressionism or the often felt influence of Whistler could do little to alter its anemic look.

Less popular at the time, but in the end more fruitful, was the example of two of America's greatest romantic realists, Winslow Homer and Thomas Eakins. We have already mentioned Homer's impressionism, but this was only one aspect of his work and its influence turned out to be the most superficial. It was rather his breadth of vision, his sense of the underlying forms in nature, his simple, forceful opposi- tions of rock and sea which had the most important effect on a new generation of painters. Eakins' influence was exerted in another sphere, that of the portrait, and in a rather different way. His style at the end of his life was darker and more soberly realist than Homer's, but it penetrated deeper into the structure of a face and the character of a sitter. Withal it had a romantic aura, often of poignancy or sadness, and a simple dignity which was monumental in its honesty and reserve. Its freer handling, in comparison with his early work, linked it partially to dark impressionism and made its influence more available to those of the Henri group. The art of both Homer and Eakins showed the way to a deeper understanding of structure and a more direct statement of natural forms. It must be emphasized, however, that in 1900 neither had yet achieved his present high reputation. Their work was very nearly lost in the prevailing sea of tonal intimacies and pyrotechnical brushwork from which it emerged but slowly.

The gradual revitalization of romantic realism in the twentieth century came first in a native search for greater breadth and monumentality. Before 1910 Rockwell Kent, a Henri student who must have known Homer's work, had already begun to paint rocks and sea in boldly simplified terms. At the same time another Henri pupil, Guy Pène du Bois, had started to do much the same thing for the human figure; from about 1908 he moved away from a Sloan-like rendering of picturesque individuals towards more generalized types of humanity which he embodied in the simplest approximation of the human form. Both lightened their palette in the direction of impressionism's higher key.

During the second decade of the century this trend began to take on the aspects of a movement. George Bellows modified the bravura style of his prize-fight pictures; his landscapes, like "The Big Dory," closely parallel Kent's work in the same field, while in his portraits he developed an Eakins-like realism and sobriety combined with a monumental composition which was partly influenced by Jay Hambidge's theory of dynamic symmetry. In the same years Eugene Speicher, Leon Kroll, and Kenneth Hayes Miller also pioneered in rendering the human body with a broad simplification of its volumes. Though plainly romantic in feeling, their art has at times an almost classical breadth and repose. It may, indeed, have been this duality of romantic intention and classical means which was later responsible for the rather mannered quality that crept into some of their work and particularly into that of their less gifted followers.

About 1920 romantic realism was more vigorously enriched by the return to its fold of a number of painters who had experimented for a time with abstraction or expressionism. Nearly all of these had become keenly aware of Cézanne's great synthesis of form and color. Reversing

**87**

the cautious formal advances of the others, they worked from a more radical art back towards a more realist one, weaving what they had learned from modernism more and more tightly into the traditional structure. Like many American artists, they realized, after the first excitement of the modern movement had passed, that they were not yet ready to express what they wanted to say in purely formal language, if indeed they ever would be. They discovered that subject was still necessary to them, that the moods of nature, the character of things and men, the sensuous appeal of the human body were still the mainsprings of their art even though they found in modernism fresher and more effective ways to embody their feeling for these.

During the early 1920's this group, quite independent of each other, went through a remarkably similar stylistic evolution. Starting under Fauve or cubist influence, they all traversed a phase when they were strongly affected by Cézanne, the Fauves emphasizing his color relations, the abstractionists his planular structure. From this they moved gradually, some more and some less, towards an increased realism in which formal values were submerged though never entirely lost.

The Fauve side of this development was represented by Bernard Karfiol and Walt Kuhn. Both had started with rather mannered elongations and distortions of the human body; both then built a more monumental figure style, Karfiol sensitively combining something of Renoir's forms with Cézanne's most delicate and complex color relations, Kuhn drawing on Cézanne's more expressionist work for his heavier forceful style. On the abstract side, Henry L. McFee, Maurice Sterne, and A. S. Baylinson had all worked in a cubist vein while Andrew Dasburg had been a Synchromist. Dasburg and McFee returned, about 1916–17, to a rather similar representational style in which objects were faceted by Cézanne's sharply defined planes to strengthen the feeling of their cubical structure and to build compositions of closely related volumes. Maurice Sterne developed more gradually in the same direction; he had never been totally abstract, but he slowly softened the angularity of his semicubist planes until, by about 1923, they also had come much closer to Cézanne in feeling. Baylinson's evolution followed approximately the same line although his exotic color and the sensuous nature of his art obscured somewhat his debt to the French master.

The Cézannesque phase through which all these men passed about 1920 was only a temporary one, however. As the decade wore on the strong formal influence of the French painter gradually disappeared from their work. Some of it was irretrievably lost but much of it became more closely integrated with their individual styles. None of them would again paint the purely visual aspects of nature without searching for its underlying structure and a meaningful relation in its parts. But while their art became more personal and more closely related to native tradition, there can be no doubt that it also lost something of its original force.

As they evolved towards an increasing realism, the work of these painters approached more and more closely that of the earlier Speicher-Kent-Kroll group until the two lines, coming from opposite directions, joined in a rapidly spreading movement. Its style, insofar as we can generalize about one which was made up of many personal variations, was broad in treatment, the volumes ample, minor details suppressed for unity of effect, the composition balanced, often static and rather monumental. Its characteristic simplifications followed two lines: one, the hard metallic surfaces of Kent, Kroll, du Bois, and Miller; the other, the slightly blurred forms (like those in a restrained soft-focus photograph) of Speicher, McFee, and to a lesser extent Kuhn and Karfiol. Their subjects tended to be conventional ones: nudes, still lifes, portraits, studio interiors, some landscapes. Because of this and their careful workmanship, they have sometimes been called the studio painters.

From about 1925, many younger artists widened greatly the scope of the style without departing far from its general character. One group explored further the soft manner of Speicher and Karfiol, utilizing their quiet, brooding figures with wide, unseeing eyes and their general mood of poetic reverie. Chief of these was Alexander Brook, who infused his enigmatic women, his lonely southern landscapes, and even his conventional still lifes with a sharper poignancy than his predecessors had achieved. Brook is also master of a subtle humor tinged with pathos, as his portraits of children testify. Closely allied to him is Raphael

Soyer, who has found on Fourteenth Street none of the colorful hurly-burly which attracted Sloan and Luks but little episodes of lonely shoppers and girls ironing in back rooms which are full of a tender and wistful sadness. These could slip easily into sentimentality were it not for his strongly knit designs, sometimes a little reminiscent of Degas. Julian Levi, who had experimented with abstraction during the 1920's, also bolstered the formal content of romantic realism in the mature style which he developed about 1934. His coastal scenes with their ragged, monumental patterns of wrecks, buoys, and drying nets have a blurred and mysterious atmosphere somewhat akin to that of the French neo-romantics. The soft focus of this group was translated by Isabel Bishop into a silvery haze which bathes her remote, impersonal figures and nearly consumes them in its delicate patina.

A more overt and vigorous romanticism informs the work of another large group, most of whom have sought to replace the static designs of the movement's early phases with dynamic motion. Reginald Marsh, particularly, has adapted the wiry, curling line of seventeenth-century baroque draftsmen to his own ends; he has also learned from them how to impose an order of sinuous, turbulent motion on large groups of figures. The frankly sexual forms and exuberant compositions of his burlesque and Coney Island scenes suggest Rubens translated into a very personal modern idiom, just as his human derelicts dwarfed beneath towering structures of "el" posts, signs, and tenement façades recall Piranesi in equally modern dress. Jon Corbino has also drawn heavily on Rubens, at one time perhaps too heavily. Fletcher Martin, during the late 1930's, developed a different kind of dynamism based on Cézanne's simplified planes which he set in motion by angular distortions. Joseph Hirsch did much the same thing, although the influence of the French master is more submerged in his vigorous native realism. Zoltan Sepeshy and Henry Schnakenberg might also be included with this group; in their different ways both have sought linear motion and fluid, interlocking designs. Many of these painters, especially Marsh, Hirsch, and Martin, have found their most characteristic subjects in the lusty, raffish, sensual life of our towns and cities. They are the spiritual, though not the stylistic, inheritors of Sloan and Luks; indeed

**90**

both Marsh and Hirsch studied under the latter. With a good many others who might be added to their number, they have formed the robust and extrovert wing of romantic realism in its later years.

This brief catalogue can only suggest the variety and the great vitality which existed during the 1930's within what might be called the main line of romantic realism. In addition, the movement spread quickly in still other directions. As early as 1920 Henry Varnum Poor had written: "Obviously present day American art must be eclectic. The art forms of every age and people are our heritage. The richness of methods is tremendous — it is almost our undoing. . ." [4] Poor himself, who had started, like the other pioneers, under a strong Cézanne influence, began at this time to introduce more pronounced expressionist elements into his work. His "Portrait of a Woman" with its forceful angular design even has a conservative resemblance to Karl Hofer's style, although it is quite possible that Poor was not then acquainted with the German expressionist's work. Poor has continued to develop an art of heavy, irregular rhythms which he varies widely in accordance with the character of his subjects. He has been joined at various times by Morris Kantor, Peppino Mangravite, Henry Mattson, and several others in the modified expressionism which constitutes this branch of romantic realism.

A quite different blend of realism with romantic-expressionist design was achieved by Thomas Benton in certain phases of his work which have had a wide influence on regional painting in America. We have already discussed Benton's more extreme style in the chapter on expressionism. Often, however, he modified his flamelike forms and twisting patterns in the direction of a much greater realism, as in his "Preparing the Bill" of 1935. His forceful work in this manner had for a time a heavy impact on the vision of such younger painters as Joe Jones and John de Martelly. It also had a parallel in the still more realistic work of John Steuart Curry, another exponent of regionalism. Unlike Benton, Curry had no strong formal concepts but depended more on the inspiration of his subject to find its appropriate embodiment. "If you feel the significance of life," he wrote, "the design builds itself." [5] His penchant for dramatic episodes, however, often led him,

**91**

as in his "Line Storm" or "Hogs Killing Rattlesnake," towards romantic distortions somewhat akin to those of Benton and his followers.

Finally, romantic realism produced two artists who, from our still short perspective, seem to have achieved the most complete and the most individual expression of the movement's aims. They are Edward Hopper and Charles Burchfield, quite unlike in most respects but akin in the depth and intensity of feeling which they have breathed into their characteristically American subjects. Perhaps it would be more accurate to speak of the feeling which their subjects have inspired in them, for they are, in a sense, the true apostles of regionalism, finding in their chosen aspects of the country a spirit which is half-local, half-universal in its humanity.

Burchfield's art, especially, is closely tied to its setting, the small towns of Ohio and the bleak back streets of Buffalo. (He has rather ironically been given a medal for having "dignified Buffalo in the eyes of the world.") In such places, during the middle years of his career — for we are not now concerned with the fantasy of his early and late periods — he found his theme of man's courage against the powers of darkness and the barrenness of provincial materialism. In his pictures the human figure is always small, often entirely absent. Actually or by implication, it is dwarfed by the dark façades of Victorian mansions and clapboard shacks which stare down with demonic window-eyes and gaping door-mouths. Or they are less obviously personified and present an aspect of bleak inscrutability. Often it is winter, the snow has turned to slush and the skies are leaden. The elements of despair are present but they seldom triumph. A lighted window glows yellow against the twilight; the small anonymous figure of a man strides unconcernedly through the slush; a tree flowers suddenly in the narrow alley between house and fence. Like *Moby Dick*, Burchfield's pictures often exist on two levels; they are transcripts of a recognizable part of American life; they are also, one may imagine, symbols of man's hope and despair. His style is well adapted to these ends. The low key, the dark shadows, the heavy, almost monotonous handling in the houses changes abruptly in his spring foliage to light, spidery patterns of branches against the sky. In his best work there is a slow, dirgelike

rhythm decorated by staccato accents and fanciful eruptions of forms.

Hopper has also painted Victorian houses with more than antiquarian interest, but it would not occur to him to see a grimacing face in the façade. More of a realist than Burchfield, he has developed a broad style of solidly defined forms and bright clear color which is closely related to the objective vision of Winslow Homer. Hopper's romanticism is one of subject rather than form; it is the product of specific experiences and places rather than the reflection of a constant attitude of mind. Much of his work, particularly his sunlit summer landscapes, is as purely objective as Homer's. But Hopper has also been acutely sensitive to those hidden tensions which exist below the level of normal human intercourse and to those nameless emotions which loneliness creates in the human spirit. Under his brush, the emptiness of a city street on Sunday morning becomes hushed and portentous. In a brightly lit office at night a business man and his secretary work after hours; a commonplace subject until one senses the conflict which Hopper has subtly created between the physical attraction of the figures and the isolating void between them. Sometimes, as James Soby has pointed out, there is the hint of an enigmatic drama in Hopper's grouping of figures.[6] "Night Hawks" may be only a picture of the bleak loneliness of a hamburg stand in the small hours of the morning; but there is also the implication of a veiled stare from the solitary figure at the left; hidden under the lowered brim, it may be only blank and unseeing; it could be more. Hopper's figures, though more individualized than Burchfield's, are much less so than Sloan's, for instance. The faces are blurred and generalized; they are those of familiar types: the clerk, the business man, the middle-aged matron. But their characters and their feelings are expressed with utmost clarity through gesture and attitude, the hunched shoulders, the droop of a head or the nervous grasp of a letter. His people are caught in the bleak, architectural settings which Hopper uses like Burchfield, though less symbolically, to reflect the oppressive forces of a material civilization. In a way it is a pessimistic art, its sense of isolation emphasized, as Parker Tyler has remarked, by the paucity of detail and the alienating quality of Hopper's light.[7] But it is only the actors in his pictures who are insensitive to the sources of

**93**

spiritual comfort which Hopper freely offers them: the cool breeze that rustles the curtain, the blue sky beyond the roof tops, and especially the brooding mystery of the city at night. For Hopper is unexcelled in evoking the mood of place and hour. His buildings are constructed with an uncanny sense of their architectural character; they are the essence of Victorian mansions, of tenements, gas stations, or summer cottages. And they exist in a palpable light and air which few artists can paint so convincingly. The infinite care and the great skill which Hopper lavishes on his settings and on some figureless pictures contributes perhaps even more than human pose and gesture to his reserved comments on the ugliness and beauty of American life.

American sculpture has also played a part, though a less prominent one, in the romantic realist movement. At the beginning of the century the pioneers in this field were a group of genre sculptors whose work paralleled in many ways the painting of the Eight. The dominant style was a pictorial one of broad modeling, impressionist treatment of planes, and a generally free and vigorous handling. It had grown out of the more meticulous nineteenth-century realism of Rogers and Remington, but its greater freedom related it perhaps more closely to the European work of Rodin and Meunier. It might also be considered with some justice as the sculptural equivalent of the dark impressionism of Luks and Bellows. With variations this was the style of Mahonri Young, Abastenia St. Leger Eberle, Charles Haag, Solon Borglum, and a good many others. To them, as to the painters, its expansive movement and warmth of surface seemed, and indeed was, ideally suited to express the excitement and fervor with which they were seeking the lively spirit of America. "I wish I could tell you," said Solon Borglum while he was still studying in Paris, "how deep in me lies this American idea; how sacred to me is the ambition to make my work typically American, to have it express the democracy, the splendid youth, the crudeness, too, if you will of my native country." [8] Something of this feeling invests the work of the whole group and had much to do, one suspects, with the deliberately rough and sketchy manner which they adopted.

From about 1930 genre sculpture received a new impetus from many younger men who have worked in a greater variety of styles. Some, like Harry Wickey, Dorothea Greenbaum, and Max Kalish, have carried forward the romantic impressionism of the earlier group, but many have further modified its realism by formal means borrowed from the various modern movements. Thus Nathaniel Kaz and Anita Weschler have used many expressionist devices such as angular planes and squat or elongated figures to intensify the emotional content of their subjects. John Hovannes has developed a fluid modeling and an open, fretwork relief construction which parallels the free forms of the abstract-surrealist group. Louis Slobodkin's small terra cottas, in spite of their topical subjects, are simplified in the direction of abstract compositions — a path which many other romantic realists have followed.

Similar variations of form, though not always as extreme, will be found in the work of those sculptors who have preferred more conventional subjects, especially the human figure or the portrait. Few of these have attempted to recreate the heroic force of Michelangelo, as George Gray Barnard did with some success in the early years of the century, but many have succumbed to the influence of Rodin's sensuous embodiment of flesh in marble. Pieces like the "Awakening Nude" of Vincent Glinsky or Oronzio Maldarelli's "Beatrice" are witness to the long persistence of the Rodin tradition, but even in these the modern sculptural tendency to compose in simplified volumes begins to temper the fleshly feeling. As one moves on to the sculpture of William Zorach, Robert Laurent, Heinz Warneke, Marion Walton, Concetta Scaravaglione, and so many other able and sensitive carvers it becomes increasingly difficult to decide whether the formal interests or those of the subject predominate. Doubtless the truth is that they are closely and inseparably balanced in the artist's mind. An animal by Warneke is replete with the character of its species, though detail is severely suppressed and not a hair breaks the nearly abstract volumes of which it is composed. The synthesis is so complete that work of this kind might have been considered with nearly equal justice in our discussion of abstraction.

Despite its tendency to blend at several points with other kinds of art, romantic realism emerges clearly enough as the dominant strain in our art from about 1925 to at least the end of the 1930's. Even today it still accounts for much of our good painting, although it has been partially engulfed in the current wave of abstraction. Its most pressing problem, however, seems to be that of the direction of its growth. And this problem has been complicated by the fact that perhaps in no other movement has so high a premium been placed on individual, idiosyncratic style. Allen Tucker once published a fable of a successful artist whose personal manner of painting became so well known that his public and his dealer refused to let him change it. So he continued to turn out the same marketable art, but privately painted for himself the kind of pictures he dreamed of doing for the public. When he finally had the courage to show these to a friend they turned out to be indistinguishable from the work which he had been exhibiting for years.[9]

There is no easy answer to this problem. In recent times we have seen both its aspects: the men who have tended to repeat more and more thinly their established styles and those who have had the courage to change abruptly, but often at the cost of losing more than they gained. On the other hand there have been artists like Hopper who have plowed the same field many times but almost always a little more deeply. And there have been others, like Burchfield, who have changed gradually, evolving an entirely different art out of elements which were latent in their established styles. Many of our romantic realists are today at such a crossroad. Whether the movement survives will depend in part on whether they can continue to grow, either by intensifying the expressive power of their existing art or by absorbing new influences and exploring new and fresh directions. This is not the only factor in the survival of the movement, however, for it is also possible that many of our young abstract painters may return again to romantic realism as McFee, Dasburg, and the rest did thirty years ago. If so it will probably be the formal lessons of Picasso and surrealism, rather than Cézanne, which will give new direction to the movement.

*descriptive & visual realism* (handwritten marginal note)

# THE TRADITION

## realists and primitives

On the technical level realism can be roughly divided into two kinds: descriptive and visual. The latter was dominant in American art at the end of the nineteenth century. In a narrow interpretation, it was the "French, or Painters' system" taught in the schools of the National Academy, which, as Professor Wilmarth said, "seeing objects in light and shade, represents them as they appear, rather than as they are." [1] It was the method of both light and dark impressionism and of the Tonalists. Descriptive realism, on the other hand, sought to render, as exactly as possible, the unchanging character of objects, their shape, texture, density, and color. It had flourished throughout the nineteenth century and has continued, or been revived, in the twentieth.

We must also distinguish between this precise, often analytical realism and the romantic realism discussed in the last chapter. In the nineteenth century the difference was clear-cut. The realists were content with the beauty of nature as they found it; like Emerson they became "a transparent eyeball" in her presence; like Burroughs they sought only "to hold the mirror of [the] mind up to Nature, that the reader may find her lineaments alone reflected there." The romantic realists, on the other hand, could point out that Emerson also demanded "in our fine arts not imitation but creation. In landscape the painter should give the suggestion of a fairer creation than we know." [2] Thus they altered and rearranged, using many formal devices which were unacceptable to the realists.

After 1900 the distinction between the two kinds of realism becomes more complex. Some of our painters have continued to find in unaltered nature an echo of the same pure poetry that the nineteenth-century landscapists revealed, but the broad and genuine pantheism of that time has largely evaporated and the innocence of the "transparent eyeball" has gone. They have been replaced partly by inward images, partly by formal values. The former have been explored by those sometimes called "magic realists," painters who, to quote Alfred Barr's definition, "by means of an exact realistic technique try to make plausible and convincing their improbable, dreamlike or fantastic visions." [3] Some of these have been strongly influenced by surrealism. Formal values have been sought by many different artists in a variety of sources, but always ones which have proved adaptable to realist ends by providing new spatial or compositional concepts without demanding distortion of the "natural" image. Some of these formal patterns have descended in an unbroken tradition from our nineteenth-century art, for even our earlier realists composed at least to the extent of selecting their point of view in a landscape and much more conspicuously in their arrangement of objects for a still life. Other designs which have lent themselves to realist treatment have been found in the deep perspective of early Renaissance painting and even in the flat designs of modern abstract art.

This formal enrichment of modern realism parallels the formal enrichment of romantic realism already discussed. But there is again a difference. The latter movement, particularly after its break with impressionism, was willing to distort the natural appearance of objects, within limits, to emphasize their structure or inner reality. The extreme realists cannot do this without the unthinkable sacrifice of the exact shape and texture of things. Cézanne's insistence on the geometrical essence of form was a logical source of inspiration for the former. It is not even available to the latter. Form, to the pure realist, means not the suppression of detail but its emphasis, sometimes even its enlargement. Design means the arrangement of these forms in a plausible but consciously contrived relation which orders life according to the vision of its creator. It is needless to add that such "pure" realism seldom exists, being often modified by more romantic values.

In the early 1900's this extreme realism had all but departed from

American art. Its greatest exponent, Thomas Eakins, was still painting but had broadened his style until it had lost the sharp precision of his earlier work. The same was true of Homer. Martin J. Heade, the last of a numerous group of mid-century landscape realists, died in 1904, but his art had long since sunk into obscurity. Cropsey, Church, and Bierstadt died between 1900 and 1902, Whittredge in 1910, carrying away the last of the Hudson River School painters. The sharply focused genre painting of Mount and Clonney had deteriorated in later hands to sentimental episodes in candy-box colors which not even the most benighted critic of the day took seriously. There was no Audubon to serve art and science with equal distinction.

One notable exception to the general eclipse of realism can be found, however. This was the long persistence of the *trompe l'oeil* tradition in our still-life painting. Founded largely by the Peales (on Dutch models) in the early nineteenth century, the deceptively realistic still life had a long and distinguished history culminating during the 1880's in the work of William M. Harnett. Harnett's extraordinary illusionistic technique and finely balanced designs were extremely popular for a time, but soon after his death in 1892 they were almost totally forgotten. Even after his rediscovery it was generally assumed that this kind of art had died with him. Recent studies by Alfred V. Frankenstein, however, have discovered a growing list of followers in the Harnett tradition — men like J. D. Chalfant, Richard Goodwin, Alexander Pope, and John F. Peto — many of whom worked well into the twentieth century.[4] Of these Peto is perhaps the most interesting. While his work lacks the dark richness and the mysterious poetry of Harnett's, it shows an even stronger sense of design, often surprisingly modern in its flat, asymmetrical patterns. It is not quite so precisely illusionistic as Harnett's, but the subtly generalized forms and the unusual color combinations contribute even more to the abstract feeling without in any way destroying the sense of closely observed reality. In recent years Hananiah Harari has revived the style with a nostalgic feeling for his Victorian objects.

We have noted elsewhere that Harnett has been claimed by the surrealists as a forerunner. While this is scarcely justified by his subjects

**99**

or intentions, there is indeed an element of mysterious significance in the sheer, trancelike intensity of his observation. On a more obvious level, he and his followers often enjoyed puns, hidden meanings, obscure allusions, and similar small mystifications. Both of these elements have been revived in recent years with more pointedly surrealist intention by the painter Walter Tandy Murch. Murch has adopted the low key and dark shadows of the Peale-Harnett work, but his freer handling and his feeling for palpable atmosphere and light is closer to Peto. His surrealist devices are not obvious, like Dali's, but are subtly intruded in almost the same sly spirit as that of the Harnett group. One looks twice before one discovers the dead beetle pinned to an odd, coral-like object on the turntable of the old phonograph. These small details underline, perhaps too obviously, the mysterious aura of his work, which is mainly achieved, as in Harnett's case, by the pure fixity of his vision. Close to Murch in technique, but quite different in feeling, are a number of academic painters such as Harry W. Watrous. They too have perpetuated the *trompe l'oeil* tradition (needless to say without surrealist overtones), but have tended to substitute more obviously "beautiful" objects — jeweled goblets and the like — for the commonplace ones of Harnett and Peto. Too often the spare strength of the earlier men is submerged in a cloying surfeit of rich and precious textures.

Harnett and his circle were almost exclusively still-life painters working within the small compass and shallow perspective of the table top or the old door. Some of the nineteenth-century realists, like Heade and Peto, did paint occasional portraits but in this field they often modified their style in a more conventional direction. One of the most interesting attempts to apply the *trompe l'oeil* technique, unchanged, to the human figure was made in the 1920's by the completely forgotten artist Frank Califano. In 1922 Califano exhibited with the Independents a "Return from a Hunt" (apparently inspired by Harnett's "After the Hunt") and in the following year, "His Master's Aim," a violin hanging on a door in the manner of Harnett's "The Old Violin." In 1924, however, he showed at the same place a painting called "Evening Usualty," in which the figure of a woman knitting replaced the conventional still life. While all these canvases have disappeared, the catalogue illustrations are clear enough to show that in humanizing his art Califano dehumanized his subject. The texture, the blemishes, the folds and wrinkles of the woman's skin are painted with such exaggerated relish that she becomes as grotesque as one's face seen in a magnifying mirror.

Califano's picture, and even his rather odd title, prefigure in a quite extraordinary way the ultimate achievement in this kind of art, which was made slightly later by the twin brothers Ivan Le Lorraine Albright and Zsissly (Malvin Marr Albright). The former, especially, has painted flesh with a repelled fascination for its cracks, pores, hairs, and wrinkles, its resemblance, as he once wrote, to "corrugated mush." [5] Beneath the surface of the skin there seem to lurk the iridescent colors of decay; they even invade the incredibly elaborate still lifes which are part of most of his pictures, and suggest the imminent dissolution of the objects. Except in the dark intensity of his vision, Albright has moved far from the Harnett tradition; the complexity and fluid motion of his arrangements may owe a slight debt to the baroque still lifes of Van Huysum or Harnett's German-American contemporary, Severin Roesen, but the dank odor, the long biblical-sounding titles, and the despairing humanity which looks out of the eyes of even his most raddled figures are entirely his own. They suggest that his motto might well be *sic transit gloria mundi.*

The *trompe l'oeil* still-life tradition is one of the few of its kind that can be shown to have persisted in an unbroken creative line from the nineteenth to the twentieth century. Nevertheless the earlier period produced several other realist movements which have recognizable parallels today, although this may be more a matter of coincidence than of continuation or conscious revival. In landscape painting, for instance, the mid-nineteenth century nourished a group of strict realists who were somewhat apart from the Hudson River School, although the studies of many of the Hudson River men (as opposed to their large exhibition pictures) were of similar character. The purest exponents of this kind of painting were Martin J. Heade and Fitz Hugh Lane. Both worked with the precision and intense observation of the still-life painters, but they were not tied to the convention of dark tones or to the latter's limited range of effects. They composed less consciously, but they played a more subtle counterpoint of solid forms against gradations of light and atmosphere. Their landscapes were always firmly constructed, sometimes with sharp, flowing contours as in Charles Herbert Moore's "The Old Bridge." The predominant feeling was quietly lyrical.

Some of these qualities began to reappear in American art in the early 1920's. Edward Bruce, who had studied Chinese painting for its rhythmical line and absorbed a Cézanne influence through Maurice Sterne, combined these diverse qualities with a natural penchant for clarity and precision. His art belongs, on the whole, with that of the romantic realists, but certain pictures, such as "A Landscape of Provence," provides a link between the work of earlier men like Moore and the strict realists of the 1930's and thereafter.

Chief of these are two young artists, Peter Hurd and Andrew Wyeth, both of whom studied with N. C. Wyeth and had their first one-man exhibitions in 1937. Hurd, who lives in New Mexico, has painted the mountains of the West with a brilliant clarity which matches that of his subject. Wyeth's technique is, at times, even more photographically exact; there is probably no more able craftsman in paint alive. Yet his aim, as he said, is "not to exhibit craft, but rather to submerge it, and make it rightfully the handmaiden of beauty, power and emotional content." [6] These he seeks partly in a heightening of natural effects, partly in subtle rearrangements which break up nature's conventional aspects. Like the work of certain modern photographers, some of his pictures are "taken" lying flat on the ground, a clump of grass near the eye looming with exaggerated size and detail against the horizon. Often, like the nineteenth-century painters, he finds the mood of his picture established by nature and requiring little assistance other than a sensitive and exact transcription. Indeed it is impossible to tell in much of Wyeth's work to what extent he has altered his original model, for his pictures are always completely plausible in a naturalistic sense. Realism of this kind, found also in the work of Ogden Pleissner, Luigi Lucioni, Dean Fausett, and a few others, comes near to establishing its own aesthetic which is only slightly formal and depends more on intensity of vision, on a complex and infinitely subtle relation of tones, textures, colors, and the like. The moment it relaxes its supreme, microscopic effort it slips easily into a tired academicism, as the less successful work of some of these men is witness.


This danger has been avoided by another and more numerous group of realists who have combined technical precision with a stronger sense of design, drawn from various sources. At their center are several artists who belonged to the Immaculate movement but who gradually permitted realism to predominate over abstract organization in their work. The abstract quality was never entirely lost, however, and continued to give even their most naturalistic paintings an underlying structural order. "There is no theoretical reason," said Louis Lozowick in a characteristic statement of their aims, "why the technical gains of abstraction cannot be used in the representation of an actual scene." There is, of course, "the danger of being so absorbed in representation as to fall into photographic actualism. Against this, however, the experience of a quarter of a century stands guard." [7]

In the late 1920's both Lozowick and Charles Sheeler began to move in this direction. Sheeler's precise and abstractly composed photographs, particularly those taken in 1927 at the Ford plant in River Rouge, exerted during the next decade their strongest influence on his work. His fascination with the complexity of machine and industrial forms culminated in his "City Interior" of 1936, a picture which marks his closest approach to a purely photographic vision. While it is not that, being doubtless a composite image, the wealth and incredible complication of detail obscure the underlying design of verticles, horizontals, and receding lines to a greater extent than in any of his other work. Toward the end of the decade he began again to paint subjects which were, both in themselves and in his treatment of them, more emphatically abstract. His "Rolling Power" of 1939 still belongs to the realist phase of his work, but it also foreshadows his return in the 1940's to his original Immaculate feeling.

Sheeler was joined, during the 1930's, by growing numbers of younger painters. Most of these have remained more faithful to realism than he, perhaps because they came directly into the movement without his long career as an Immaculate behind them. At the same time, all have incorporated elements of abstract design in their work and several have followed closely Sheeler's choice of industrial subjects. Edmund Lewandowski has been, until recently, the closest to Sheeler's realist phase. Raised in Milwaukee, he has lived intimately with machines and factories since childhood and still finds more beauty, he has said, in a row of ventilators than in one of country trees. These he has painted in remarkably solid water colors which make the most of rhythmical repetitions and variations. There is a more romantic and personal note in the machines of Theodore Lux Feininger (who has also painted under the name of Theodore Lux). Feininger has preferred old wood-burning locomotives and side-wheel steamers with their archaic aura of a more innocent past. His precision has a hint of stiffness in it, a scarcely audible echo of our nineteenth-century primitives and chromolithographs. There is a warmth, a sentiment, a nostalgia in his work which is seldom found among the pure realists.

This kind of hard, Immaculate-related realism has been carried by others into the more conventional fields of landscape, still life, and figure painting. Alexandre Hogue has used it effectively to portray the desolation wrought by wind and erosion in the dust bowl of the southwest. John Rogers Cox has applied it to the grain fields of the plains and other subjects. Two women, Katherine Schmidt and Audrey Buller, have softened it a little, enriched its textures, and used it to express more intimate emotions, but both have kept something of its rectilinear design and spare simplicity.

The same qualities have also informed a new school of genre painting which began to emerge about 1930. In that year Grant Wood painted his now famous "American Gothic," a picture of detailed realism in a severely frontal, monumental design. Wood diverged into a sterile primitivism, but a few years later the style was reforged with quite different feeling by two New York painters, Paul Cadmus and Jared French. Cadmus' metallic realism gave America a shock, for he has used it to probe with unsparing detail some of the most sordid aspects of urban life, especially sex relations at a purely physical level. In part his intentions have been avowedly satirical, but it is difficult to accept his pictures as satires, partly because his characters are so little exaggerated in the direction of types, partly because his interest in them always seems one of curious fascination rather than pity or indignation. Stylistically, Cadmus is a knowing and eclectic composer. Unlike the Immaculates he has ranged beyond the severe patterns of abstract art and has borrowed many elements of design from the Renaissance and the other great traditions of Western art. He has made these very much his own, selecting and modifying them with an instinctive feeling for the exact requirements of his subjects.

Cadmus has inspired a number of other painters who, without his intensity of vision and feeling, have produced only gross and tawdry comments on the adolescent mentality of some Americans. His one close rival today seems to be the young painter Henry Koerner, who has developed independently an art remarkably similar to that of Cadmus in many ways. He has not dealt with quite such controversial themes but his characters have often been as profoundly bestial, in the literal meaning of the word. Again no moral emerges — only a kind of fascination, which is somehow slyer than Cadmus' frank interest. Koerner is still very young and may change greatly; already he has an extraordinary technical ability and his extensive formal borrowings from the past, like those of the older artists, are intelligently integrated in his personal style.

A number of other painters are more loosely allied to this new genre movement. Jared French shows technical and compositional similarities to Cadmus, but the cool archaism of his figures and the deep space through which he often views them give his art a remote, impersonal quality. At times he has even invoked surrealist images and symbols, as in his "Murder." This has also been done by Louis Guglielmi, but with an entirely different feeling. Guglielmi has acknowledged his debt and kinship to Demuth, Dickinson, and Sheeler; his painting, in both its realist and surrealist phases, is much closer to the Immaculates in its quasi-geometrical design than it is to Cadmus or French. It differs from all these in its warm compassion for humanity; even Guglielmi's fan-

**105**

tastic devices are used objectively to underline his sympathy with the city's poor rather than to dredge up autobiographical secrets.

With Guglielmi we return to a more purely Immaculate vision modified in the direction of surrealism. This trend was first and most forcibly seen in the work of Peter Blume, who had started his career during the late 1920's as a typical Immaculate in the Demuth-Sheeler manner. In 1930–1932, however, Blume painted three pictures, "Parade," "South of Scranton," and "Light of the World," which transformed his art into a pure fantasy of human figures enigmatically trapped in odd arrangements of the machine forms dear to the Immaculates. Since then he has moved slowly away from a mechanistic vision, intensifying his realism and exploring the greater variety of textures and organic forms of nature. In his studies and smaller pictures these are often purely fantastic and sometimes erotic in a typically surrealist fashion. But in "The Rock," his one major composition of the last twelve years, they are disciplined in the service of a vast allegory — surely one of the most extraordinary pictures of our day. Blume stands alone in the single-minded intensity of what James Soby has perceptively called his "ruthless introspection," [8] but while he has had no followers, there has been a "Postsurrealist" movement, founded in California in 1934 by Lorser Feitelson, Helen Lundeberg, and others, which has also produced some precisely realist work of abstract design and surrealist feeling.

Finally, still another kind of realism has flourished here which is harder to define than those branches which grew from the Immaculate trunk. Its chief characteristic is its debt to primitive art, such as the drawings of children, the pictures of "Sunday painters," or the work of the early Renaissance. Like the sources on which it draws, it is not visually exact or photographic, but seeks a direct, naïve apprehension of reality. It is an emotional rather than a technical realism, for the meaning of objects rather than their actual shape determines the pictorial form. On occasion it also owes something to modern abstract design, which indeed parallels primitive art in certain respects.

**106**

The leading figure in this movement since the middle 1930's has been Ben Shahn. While he has drawn on various primitive sources, Shahn's art is perhaps closest to that of children in its sensitive linear quality, its deliberate awkwardness, its often humorous conventions for noses or mouths. This is obvious in such pictures as "Ohio Magic" with its childlike charabanc and each cobblestone drawn with persistent care and a plain disregard for diminishing perspective. But even in paintings where it is less apparent, such as the poignant "Father and Child," it is at the center of Shahn's unclouded vision of human suffering and dignity. It is not, of course, his only formal means, for he is a master of abstract design, be it in depth like that of Uccello or di Chirico, or flatly two-dimensional like that of Piero della Francesca or Diego Rivera. He also uses, occasionally, expressionist distortions of form and perspective, particularly in his posters. His personal convictions on social justice have involved him deeply in painted propaganda, some of which ranks high in his work. But it is in his easel pictures that he has captured most purely the feeling of humility and wonder which the stubborn endurance of the human spirit so patently wakens in him.

Shahn's art has had a growing influence on several younger painters, such as Bernard Perlin. Few, however, have maintained the older man's three-way balance between a tough-minded realism, a sophisticated design, and an ingenuous vision; Perlin, for instance, is both more delicate and more romantic. Stephen Greene, another young artist who emerged in the 1940's, resembles Shahn chiefly in his more obvious dependence on the early Renaissance for the primitive element in his style; his first religious pictures had the eloquent simplicity of their source, translated into a modern and personal idiom, but since then he seems to be developing in a somewhat different direction. Perhaps the closest to Shahn in feeling, though not in style, is Honoré Sharrer whose art is also concerned with the intimate lives of working people. These she would like to render "with fanatical sensitivity and creative realism"; [9] and to this end she has developed the most precisely realistic technique of any of the painters in this group. But she has also given her pictures a fresh and ingenuous air by posing many of her

**107**

figures in slightly stiff, self-conscious attitudes as if they were well aware that their likeness was being taken. Her work hints at the archaic charm of old daguerreotypes or those primitive portraits by the anonymous limners of the nineteenth century.

The primitivism of all these painters is an important but an elusive element in their work; it is not as eclectic as it sounds for it has been deeply absorbed into their personal way of seeing and painting. This has not always been the case, however. Other artists, like Lucille Corcos, have consciously imitated the quaint mannerisms of the Sunday painter, or, like Florine Stettheimer, the naïve drawings of children, to create an art which is gay and fanciful but highly mannered.

We have also had, throughout the last half century, those genuine primitives, or untrained artists, whose timeless patterns of seeing have changed so little during the history of our art. While they have not the technical skill to transcribe the outward appearance of nature, their work is generally realistic in intent and obviously inspired by an urge to record with loving care those subjects which have emotional significance for them. It is true that at times the emotional content of a subject is so great that it forces the artist into a kind of primitive expressionism, as in the brooding, introspective "Self-Portrait" of John Kane. The more usual mood, however, is placid and idyllic: the fond contemplation of a familiar scene, like Joseph Pickett's "Manchester Valley," or of imaginary visions like Horace Pippin's "The Holy Mountain." "Pictures just come to my mind," Pippin once said, "and then I tell my heart to go ahead." [10]

Through all this work, as well as in that of "Grandma" Moses, Morris Hirshfield, and so many others, there is a constant quality of rhythmical, flat design which seems, in varying degrees, to be an innate and universal part of our vision.

# 9

## THE TRADITION

### romantic visionaries

It is not quite accurate to speak of a tradition of romantic and visionary art in America, for the nineteenth-century painters who fall under this heading were generally isolated figures pursuing the private images of their imagination. Since 1800, however, there has never been a time when one or more was not active: first Allston, then Quidor and Blythe, and at the end of the century Ryder, Blakelock, and Newman — to mention only the outstanding figures. They founded no movements and, as far as we know, drew no sustenance from each other. But taken together, they wove a continuous thread of reverie and melancholy, of fantasy and terror and intimate poetry through the more prosaic texture of our earlier art. Their tradition is one of mood rather than style, for in the latter they differed greatly, uniting only in their common rejection of realism as an end in itself. They rejected also, at various times, other current aesthetic beliefs. Thus Allston fashioned an idealistic art when it was scarcely known in America; yet when idealism became dominant, Quidor and Blythe denied it with their robust and earthy subjects; and when idealism vanished before late-century materialism, it was revived again by Ryder, Blakelock, and Newman. Their tradition was one of independence and revolt, as well as mood.

In the twentieth century, we have had as many poets of the inner eye, but their relation to the rest of our art has changed greatly. For the first time in our history, the influence of one or two dominant figures has been felt soon enough and strongly enough to establish what might, with a little exaggeration, be called a movement. Much more important has been the disruption of realist standards by abstract art since early in the century. Although the imaginative artist is often unsympathetic to abstraction, he owes it a debt for lightening his isolation and making possible a greater freedom of expression. Finally, the advent of surrealism in the 1930's has almost abolished the distinction between the romantic visionary and those who seek the fantastic images of the subconscious mind. A distinction does exist, however, for the art of the former is less egocentric (relatively speaking) and tends to find its mysteries in things, in nature, and ultimately in God. Again, as in the nineteenth century, our romantic visionaries have worked in a variety of styles, now further enlarged by the influence of the various modern movements, but formal values have continued to be a means rather than an end and have been closely tailored to the nature of their visions.

During the opening years of the twentieth century, the prevailing mood in this kind of art was one of gentle and idyllic reverie often tinged with sadness. The greatest of our romantic visionaries, Albert Pinkham Ryder, was still painting until shortly before his death in 1917, although his inspiration flagged after 1900 and his chief labor was directed to perfecting and refinishing his earlier canvases. Ryder had explored turbulent and awe-inspiring themes in his "Flying Dutchman" and other pictures of supernatural events, but he was also the painter of tranquil moonlit marines and pastoral Arcadian landscapes. There was mystery in these, but it was a peaceful mystery without the dark terror of his greatest works. In all of them there was the sure and forceful design, the strange arabesques of cloud forms and land forms, the generally dark tonality, the art of the half-hidden, half-revealed.

Ryder's work began to exert some influence at this time. Among his early admirers were Benjamin Kopman and a group of young painters who called themselves the Introspectives. In 1917, the year of Ryder's death, they issued a manifesto written by Jennings Tofel which was "a protest against superficial surface art . . . a plea for . . . insight, feeling, imagination." [1] Mrs. Gertrude Vanderbilt Whitney gave them an exhibition and another was arranged at Knoedler's.

**110**

In addition to Tofel and Kopman they included Abraham Harriton and Claude Buck. The sculptor Robert Laurent and several younger painters were invited to exhibit with them, also the somewhat older Van Dearing Perrine, who spent his winters in hermitlike seclusion in a deserted church and school building at the foot of the Palisades. Ten years earlier Perrine had told John Spargo, "To imitate the outward and visible forms of nature . . . does not make the slightest appeal to me. . . The whole world appears to me as one vast miracle, and I am part of the whole. . . What I try to do is to register a principle, to express something of that deep reverent emotion, using such forms as seem to me best fitted to convey the solemn grandeur of it to others." [2]

Perrine's art at this time was gently mystical in an Oriental manner which owed a great deal to Japanese prints. To the younger painters, however, Ryder was a more fertile source of inspiration. Kopman, especially, was profoundly influenced by Ryder's dark, irregular patterns which he used in a rather personal way that often suggested additional infusions of Delacroix, Redon, or even the Fauves. Another aspect of Kopman's early work, seen in such pictures as "Interior" — a featureless woman in a dark and gloomy hovel — is closer to Eugene Higgins than to Ryder. But Higgins, in spite of his social realism, might well be included with this group for his emphasis was predominantly on the spiritual suffering of man and there is a strong mystical and religious current in his work. Somewhat later this was again revived by Fred Nagler.

The reveries of the early century were not always conceived in darkness and touched with melancholy. By 1900 Arthur B. Davies had developed a fragile and idyllic art on the twin themes of childhood and legend, although neither of these are precise descriptions. His children, who dance or stroll or gaze wonderingly at the sea, are as one-sided in their purity and innocence as those of Robert Louis Stevenson, whom they resemble to a marked degree. His legends are enigmatic and seldom related to literary ones. Nude and faintly classical maidens float in dancelike rhythm across the surface of his long, narrow pictures, which often suggest Grecian friezes. They are the least

**111**

fleshly nudes in American art, and they grew even more ethereal after 1922 when Davies became interested in Gustavus A. Eisen's theory of inhalation and released them, by their indrawn breaths, from the laws of gravity. Davies' idealized visions come perilously close to a cloying sweetness; their genuine poetry, like that of *A Child's Garden of Verses*, depends on the willingness of the spectator to withdraw into a sexless, immaterial world where beauty is unrelieved by poignancy or pain.

The same mannered nudes and enigmatic subjects are also found in the weirder visions which Middleton Manigault recorded during the few productive years of his career between about 1909 and 1919. But here the similarity ends, for Manigault's figures, in spite of their stylized and decorative poses, are subtly erotic with narrow waists, large hips and breasts. There is a studied incongruity between their flesh-and-blood existence and their meaningless occupations in the fairy-tale landscapes which contain them. Titles like "Source," "Tide," and "Galaxy" deepen the ambiguity. Manigault also painted pure landscapes, such as "A Town in France" with its almost Cézannesque feeling for the cubical essence of architecture, but even in this field he preferred imaginative compositions like "The Prison," which contrasts an idyllic foreground of swans and grazing horses with the gloomy bastion on the hill. His style owed much to primitive art, which he sometimes recreated almost verbatim, as in "A Pastoral" or "Wooden Indian." About 1919 he changed direction entirely and in the next few years painted some two hundred cubist pictures, which he subsequently destroyed. One wonders what his mature synthesis of form and imaginative fancy might have been had he not died, in 1922, at the age of thirty-five.

The Land of Cockaigne which Davies and Manigault created in their different ways exists with more sensuous reality in the work of our tortured and eccentric visionary, Louis M. Eilshemius, self-styled supreme Parnassian, Mightiest All-Round Man, Transcendant Eagle of Art, inventor of electric belts, homeopathic procedures, and hypnotic spells. Beneath the egotism and the hocus-pocus of his utterances, there was a sensitive and mystical spirit which desperately sought relief from its frustrations in images of a South Sea paradise, like that of Melville's *Typee*, or in a rustic America as idyllic as Davies' child world. These were not entirely imaginary, for Eilshemius had been to Samoa in 1901, as well as to many other romantic corners of the world. But his pictures are not the reports of a traveler; they are retreats from civilization which he has prepared for himself, full of wanton joys for the body in the South Sea pictures, full of a childlike innocence and simplicity in "A Bridge for Fishing" and similar country scenes. Sometimes the fantasy is more obvious; his nude maidens in "Afternoon Wind" angle through the air as if propelled by an indiscreet application of Davies' theory of inhalation. But for the most part Eilshemius created a plausible world which is unreal only because it is so pure a reflection of his own impossible desires. His style was perfectly adapted to his purpose, for it combined something of Ryder's mysterious patterning with a naïve, almost childlike draftsmanship which underlined the subjective nature of his visions. These entered darker realms, too, as we shall see later.

The fragile irreality of Davies and Manigault, of some part of Eilshemius, and even of Ryder's little shepherdesses or his "Forest of Arden" was as typical of one side of the American mind in the early twentieth century as the futurists' mechanistic dynamism was of a diametrically opposed feeling. Both were, to some extent, reactions in different directions to the waxing clamor of our industrial civilization, which the futurists embraced and the visionaries fled. Both have largely disappeared from our art today, though never entirely so. Perhaps the closest inheritor of the gently idyllic strain has been the young painter Raymond Breinin who, unlike his predecessors, has made the city itself into a place of magic full of moonlit visions, winged horses, and childhood memories of the steeples of Vitebsk. Yet there is a difference, for Breinin's art is more international in flavor, with reminiscences of El Greco's attenuated figures and the Russian folk fantasy of Chagall. It is in his less extravagantly imaginative pictures that he comes closest to the native tradition.

Two slightly older men, John Carroll and Hobson Pittman, have also added to our modern vein of quiet reverie. Carroll's darkly dreaming maidens, though not so securely virginal as Davies', are caught in the same hypnotic trance, their creamy flesh more sensual but nearly as bloodless. Pittman's haunted Victorian parlors also exist in a light-suffused trance; the ghosts have slipped from sight and for a moment everything is poised and hushed in expectation. The minor poetry of these men is real, but the narrowness of their chosen fields has made it difficult for them to maintain consistently the freshness of mood which one finds in their best work.

As the plausible, if Utopian, visions of these men have dwindled, a darker, more mysterious romanticism which believes in good and evil miracles has grown. It too had its roots in the work of Ryder, particularly in the majestic canvases of supernatural events: "Death on a Pale Horse," "Jonah," "The Flying Dutchman," "Macbeth and the Witches." If we add to these some of Ryder's more eerie landscapes, such as "Smugglers' Cove," we have the three main strands in this kind of art: the mysteries of God, of nature, and of evil. In various ways they have obsessed the imagination of growing numbers of our painters.

About 1908 Louis Eilshemius called on Ryder in his cluttered studio and saw there two of his greatest pictures, "The Flying Dutchman" and "Macbeth and the Witches." With the courage of his peculiar egotism, Eilshemius undertook his own versions of the same subjects, which were to surpass those of the older artist. While he did not succeed, his pictures have a different kind of strength — less ample than Ryder's but full of the narrow intensity of their author. In several subsequent pictures, which sprang more directly from his own painful experience, Eilshemius returned to themes of suffering and evil. His "Jealousy" of 1915, though wildly melodramatic, distills the bitter essence of its subject with nightmare force.

One year after this picture was painted, a twenty-three-year-old artist in Salem, Ohio, was doubtfully commencing a series of water colors which are among our most haunted visions since those of Ryder. Returning from the Cleveland School of Art to the village where he had grown up, Charles Burchfield was drawn by an obscure inner compulsion "back into childhood memories, and it became such an obsession that a decadence set in. I tried to recreate such moods as fear of the dark, the feelings of flowers before a storm, and even to visualize the songs of insects and other sounds." [3] The marvels and the terrors of childhood blossom in Burchfield's strange images and anthropomorphic forms. The church steeple is a monstrous dragon, the "Night Wind" is a cloud and a witch in one, the "First Hepaticas" bloom in a wood of threatening shapes and gaping hollow trees. Or the mood changes to the jubilant springtime of the Psalms: "And the little hills rejoice on every side . . . they shout for joy, they also sing." Sunflowers are a "Rogues Gallery"; shrill insects fill the air with staccato marks. Nature has seldom been more imaginatively personified.

Not the least remarkable feature of these water colors is the inventive style in which they are painted. Certain elements such as the sharply peaked roofs and dripping walls of his buildings or the witch face in a cloud seem drawn in a very general way from an international fairy-tale convention; at least they are in the spirit of the brothers Grimm. There is also a fainter kinship with Ryder, whose work Burchfield probably did not know at this time, in the abstract patterns of cloud and night shapes. Certainly he was entirely unaware of the force lines of the futurists when he painted spring trees and foliage in sharply aspiring chevrons or outbursts of sinuous curves, although he may have seen reproductions of Oriental art with its comparable shorthand for leaves and branches. Whatever his sources, Burchfield created a remarkably mature and personal style for so young a painter. From 1918 through the decade of the thirties he laid it aside for the more sober realism which we have already discussed, but in recent years it has served him again as he has returned once more to fanciful speculations on nature. Indeed he has found it so well suited to his needs that he has altered it little; on occasion he has even enlarged his early papers, using them as the center of more complex compositions which he works out in the added margins.

Burchfield's work of 1916–1918 was forgotten or unknown for many years; even his own reference to it, quoted above, had a half-apologetic ring. Yet it is an unusual coincidence that several other painters with a romantic and visionary bent have, since then, arrived independently at styles which parallel Burchfield's patterns of weird and flamelike forms, though they have generally avoided his hidden faces and the like. Oscar Bluemner's "Moonshine Fantasy," painted sometime before 1929, is perhaps the closest to Burchfield in feeling; though more heavily romantic, its fluid design of trees and building is filled with the same supernatural magic. On a somewhat more decorative level, the religious pictures of Augustus Vincent Tack have also used wavering and elusive shapes like Pentecostal fire. Finally, and more important than these, the abstract nature lyrics of Arthur G. Dove freed themselves during the early 1940's from the heavier forms of his previous work and began to dance and flicker in purely fantastic images which suggest the shapes of organic growth, the roll of waves, the flash of lightning, and similar disembodied forces of nature. As Duncan Phillips has pointed out, Dove was a visionary and a poet in the Ryder tradition.[4] But he was also an artist of a different century. Like Burchfield, his art has that sharper, more nervous intensity which is doubtless the mark of our times, just as the more unbridled fancies of both men could have found expression only in a period no longer dominated exclusively by realist standards.

The work of all these artists is remotely linked to that of Ryder in its use of fluid abstract forms derived from those of nature and in its search for a pictorial embodiment of mysterious forces. But Ryder has had even more direct successors in several other painters who have been less deliberately fantastic, who have stayed closer to the moods and shapes of nature herself, though like him they have found their own ways to intensify these. On the West coast, Matthew Barnes, after years of self-taught experiment, developed in the mid thirties a Ryderesque art of moonlit, ghostly houses often perched on vertiginous peaks. It is a kind of vertical equivalent to the older painter's horizontal seas. Also largely self-taught is the New York artist Paul Mommer; in the back room of the beauty parlor which has provided his living he has painted in his spare time private visions, full of the somber dusk of evening or the looming, half-revealed forms of night. Superficially, Elliot Orr's work of a few years ago is even closer to that of Ryder in its patterned skies and stormy seas; but there is a nervous intensity in Orr's ragged edges and the fragmentation of his designs which differentiates them sharply from the older artist's ample and majestic patterns.

The human figure played a relatively small role in the work of Ryder; with a few notable exceptions it is absent or it appears as an indistinguishable shadow which serves to emphasize the lonely vastness of the scene. This is also true, in general, of the artists we have discussed above. In contrast to them, two Western painters, C. S. Price and Kenneth Callahan, have created a darkly mystical art in which man, though seldom individualized, is often the protagonist. Both owe much to modern abstract art and both have been concerned — Callahan consistently, Price occasionally — with man's ambiguous relation to God and to the world. Here the similarity ends, for Price works in a blocky, monumental style which seems vaguely related to Rouault's somber mysticism; Callahan in a fluid, baroque manner, weaving his rather Blake-like figures into strained and shifting patterns. In the heavy gravity of the one and the tortured imagination of the other we have two divergent types of the romantic visionary: one which wonders and accepts, the other which wonders and rebels.

All art of this kind is subjective, but within that general term there are many degrees. In Ryder, in Dove, even in Burchfield and Eilshemius there is a universal quality which partly transcends the privacy of their inner musings. Their mysteries are cosmic ones which surround us all, their subjects are ample enough to touch the experience of every man who is capable of wonder. The night, the sea, the forest, and the wind are the large and visible manifestations of a spiritual force and contain within themselves the essence of the miraculous. It is no accident that they recur again and again in the romantic visions of the present as well as those of the past.

Within the last fifteen or twenty years, however, a new and more deeply subjective vein has been explored by several of our painters, who might be called the intimate poets of the romantic vision. The difference between their art and that of the others is not a question of subject alone, although they have often tended to isolate small fragments of the world and to find their miracles in microcosms rather than in the larger aspects of nature. Yet the distinction does not lie here, for they have also sought the general mysteries of moonlight, forest, and sea. Rather it depends on the privacy of their vision, on the intensity of personal meaning which they have found in external things and embodied in intimate symbols that are yet related to a larger spiritual truth. It is a question whether their art could have existed before surrealism opened the avenues of introspection, but whatever it may owe to that movement has been largely submerged in the course of its quite different quest.

Two of the leading figures in this kind of art, Mark Tobey and Morris Graves, share a mystical and religious fervor which has drawn sustenance from Oriental thought, as their art has drawn also on the Far East for a certain calligraphic quality. Even before 1920 Tobey was deeply interested in automatic writing with the planchette, but it was not until after a trip to China in 1934 that he developed the style by which he is now best known, the semi-automatic "white writing" which enmeshes his hidden, evocative images in an endless web of incredibly complicated lines. Sometimes the image is part of the web, as in his "Drift of Summer"; sometimes it lies behind it or is intertwined with it, as in "Island Memories" or "Tundra." But in either case the shimmering network creates a remote, unearthly splendor like the endlessly varied and repeated rhymes of Poe's poetry or the patterns that float behind the eyelids when they are suddenly closed in sunlight.

Graves, who came under Tobey's influence about 1938, has made occasional use of the same device, but has used it less abstractly, often to denote the moonlight which weaves its enchanted linear spells around the birds and snakes of his nocturnal world. For Graves is more of a realist than Tobey and even when he paints that composite and obsessive creature, the "Little Known Bird of the Inner Eye," it is instinct with the character of better-known species. This realism, or rather this acuteness of observation, is necessary to the magic symbols which Graves creates; it is part of the terrible pathos of his blind and wounded creatures; it is what gives his very small "Bird Singing in the Moon-light" its moving bravery in the lonely night. Half-real, half-hallucina-tory, his concentrated images have, in James Soby's words, "an uncanny sense of privacy, as though they had not been witnessed by the painter, but had been recorded on enchanted film by shutters tripped in the primeval dark, with no one near." [5]

A more lightly fanciful bestiary has been created by Darrel Austin in richly crusted canvases built up entirely with the palette knife. His forlorn maidens lost in swamps with their bulls, foxes, tigers, cata-mounts, and strange birds have the same irreality and the same obscurely legendary look as those of Arthur B. Davies, though none of the latter's sweetness and light. Indeed they are closer to surrealism than the work of most of this group, for Austin has said that he usually starts a picture with no conception of what its subject will be and permits it to evolve from subconscious promptings.[6]

More than any of the others, Loren MacIver has captured the magic in the small commonplace things of life. Her unqualified state-ment, "Quite simple things can lead to discovery," is one key to her art.[7] In a blistered pavement, the fading chalk marks of a hopscotch game, or the discarded treasures of an ashcan, she finds the poignant records of life's passing joys; obliquely, serenely, they recall the lost laughter of children and the affection that once found use and beauty in rejected things. Her prevailing mood is warmly human, poetic, a little mystical; her method, like that of Graves, varies widely from sharply focused realism to near abstraction. The delicate balance of humor and sadness in her clown portraits, the flickering illumination in her rows of votive lights, or the gleaming branches of a tree in winter mist are spiritual manifestations that shine through corporeal existence. Much of her work, especially the gouaches done on black paper, is subtly phosphorescent, the deep colors glowing, like those of Austin but more gently, with an other-worldly light.

Many more artists, several of whom we have discussed elsewhere, might with some justice be linked to these, for the sense of mystery is perhaps more widespread today than it has ever been, at least in our arts. The relation of such abstract painters as Stamos, Baziotes, and

Rothko to Arthur G. Dove was pointed out in Chapter VI. In like manner, the complicated linear abstractions of Jackson Pollock bear a certain resemblance to those of Mark Tobey, while the magical nature symbols of Adolph Gottlieb or Knud Merrild are fairly close to those of Morris Graves, especially in the latter's early "Message" series. The dividing line between those who have embraced wholeheartedly a romantic mysticism and those who have tempered its dominion with formal or other interests cannot be drawn with any degree of precision.

# 10

## THE ARTIST IN THE MODERN WORLD

In 1823 the poet James Gates Percival, writing to a friend of the failure of Morse's great canvas of "The House of Representatives," remarked: "He labored at it eighteen months, and spent many hundred dollars in its execution; and now he has to pay the public for looking at it. Allston says it is a masterpiece of coloring and perspective. Who would write or paint any good thing for such a *fashionable vulgar* as ours? For my part, I am tired of patting the dogs. I will now turn to kicking them." [1]

"And behold the wealthy American patrons of the arts!" wrote Benjamin De Casseres nearly a century later. "Ring Olympus with thy laughter! They carry their exhausted souls to Europe and buy 'art objects' the great money value of which they are made to appreciate . . . Stupidity and Vulgarity, thy name is America!" [2]

We must try to see in perspective the schism which has always existed, to some extent, between the American artist and his public since at least the first quarter of the nineteenth century. Those who blame the "modern" artist for his failure to meet their needs and for thus creating the breach overlook the fact of its long duration. Especially they overlook the fact that popular indifference to the fine arts has at all times forced certain American artists to work out their own salvation outside the narrow field of public taste. "Here we see the arts developing and expanding themselves, not in the genial sunshine of wealth and patronage, but in the cold damp shade of neglect and obscurity," said the *Analectic Magazine* in 1815, and it concluded, of our artists, "Their productions are, of course, somewhat adapted to the character and habits of the nation . . . yet they have always rather led than followed the public taste." "No," said the *Nation* eighty-seven years later, "The public does not really care for art — that is the truth of it." [3]

Two circumstances contributed to the steady growth of the schism in the nineteenth century: one — materialism — was constant; indeed it increased greatly at the century's end; the other — a narrow aesthetic standard — changed character but was never broad enough to contain all the creative work being done at a given time. This does not mean that no creative work was done within the current limits of public taste. For many years before the Civil War the painters of the Hudson River School met successfully the twin standards of realism and idealism then dominant; later Homer, Inness, Duveneck, and others found ample support for their respective kinds of impressionism. Yet we must remember in each period the many neglected and despised figures, not only the romantic visionaries like Quidor, Ryder, and Blakelock whose art so obviously flouted the dominant realist standard, but even the extreme realists like Heade, Lane, and Eakins who fared better but were not granted their full due because their work failed to meet other specifications.

Under the twin pressures of indifference and misunderstanding, many of our earlier artists either gave up art or withdrew from the main stream of American life in one way or another and cultivated their private gardens in relative isolation. Morse turned to science, Quidor to farming. Homer became a recluse on the Maine coast, Ryder in the city. Eakins retired to a narrow circle of family and friends, Blakelock to an insane asylum. Whistler, Cassatt, Sargent, Vedder, Currier, and scores of others became expatriates living out their lives in London, Paris, Rome, or Munich where sooner or later they faced the inescapable dilemma of Henry James: that one could not remain an American nor become an Englishman but must remain forever suspended between two cultures.

The twilight mood of much American art in the latter years of the nineteenth century is partly, one suspects, a reflection of the breach between the country and her artists. Uprooted or forced into a spiritual

isolation, many painters turned their eyes inward in melancholy introspection. They recall James's heroine in *The Portrait of a Lady* when
"the truth of things, their mutual relations, their meaning, and for the
most part their horror, rose before her with a kind of architectural
vastness. . . All purpose, all intention was suspended; all desire, too."
In the brooding sadness of a face by Eakins or the enigmatic reverie
of a figure by Dewing, we might well be looking at Isabel Archer,
who is so often posed in an attitude betraying "a singular absence of
purpose; her hands, hanging at her sides, lost themselves in the folds
of her black dress; her eyes gazed vaguely before her." In the landscapes
of Blakelock, Homer Martin, Ryder, J. F. Murphy, Inness (in his
late years); in the "Nocturnes" of Whistler, the ideal heads of Hunt,
and the religious pictures of Newman, the mood recurs. Of the great
figures, perhaps only Homer escaped entirely, although many lesser
men like Sargent and Chase, whose art was closer to the material
standards of the day, were of course untouched. While it is too sweeping a generalization, there is still much truth in the words Claude
Phillips wrote in 1902. The keynote to the art of this period, he said,
that is, to "the art which is neither official, fashionable, nor commercial
is sadness, heart-searching, misgiving, melancholy — now spiritual,
now sensuous — revolt against surrounding circumstance." [4]

On the whole, the American public remained pleasantly unaware
of this schism until the early years of the twentieth century. There
were no organized revolutionary movements, as in France, to shake its
confidence in the established order or to force a revision of values.
Even impressionism, here, slipped quietly in the back door, barely
ruffling the calm of our Olympian critics. Our Quidors and Blakelocks,
the true nonconformists, managed to starve in decent obscurity. The
National Academy, though briefly challenged by the Society of
American Artists, continued an autocratic dominion over the arts.

In the last forty years all this has changed. The exhibition of the
Eight in 1908 gave the public its first inkling that organized revolt
was possible and drew the defensive epithets already noted. But it was
of course the Armory Show of 1913 which first stirred the American
mind to an awareness of the fact that an art which it did not like or

understand could exist in the proportions of a serious movement and could not be consigned, like an individual, to oblivion. At first the conservative critics tried. By calling the modernists madmen, charlatans, and poseurs perhaps they could be effectively discouraged. When this failed America realized for the first time that a breach between it and its creative artists existed. It blamed this on the perversity of the modernist, failing to realize that a schism had existed for nearly one hundred years before, failing also to realize that we, as a people, might be more to blame than any possible artistic aberration.

If the Armory Show brought this schism into the open and made it seem more marked, it was also an important step in its healing — a process still far from complete. Momentarily, the breach was widened; the artist was confirmed in his belief that he must paint for himself alone, the public in its distrust of all deviations from academic standards. But already one persistent cause of the divorce was partially removed. The public might not be able to understand, but at least it was not indifferent. And as curiosity grew, more and more men of good will made the effort to meet the artist on his own ground, just as many artists eventually made the effort to return modernism to forms more closely related to native tradition and hence more understandable. Thus by a process of advance and retreat, of experiment and consolidation, of action and reaction, American art finally caught up with and entered the main stream of international art, at the same time bearing with it certain native qualities and a growing public interest and understanding. We must now examine some of the forces, agencies, and implications in this struggle.

Aside from his art itself, the knottiest problem for the American modernist in the early years of the century was where to exhibit. The annual exhibitions of the National Academy of Design were still the principal medium; in how many biographies one reads sentences like Lloyd Goodrich's concerning Weber: "He submitted work to a National Academy exhibition and was of course rejected, and never tried again." [5] The commercial galleries, not so numerous then as now, were equally hostile to anything as unprofitable as modern art, though some could be rented if an artist had the money, which few did. The one exception was Alfred Stieglitz's Photo-Secession Gallery, also known as the Little Gallery or 291, because of its address on Fifth Avenue. In its small room, beginning in 1908, Americans saw the first exhibitions of work by the leading French modernists and of the primitive African sculpture and children's drawings in which they were interested. From 1909 on Stieglitz showed the work of many pioneer American modernists: Bluemner, Carles, Dove, Macdonald-Wright, Marin, Maurer, Nadelman, O'Keeffe, Weber, and others. With some, like Marin, he made financial arrangements which permitted the artist to devote his entire time to painting without immediate concern for sales. His messianic zeal, supported by a sharp wit and tongue, did much to weld the isolated efforts of the early men into a cohesive movement. Their almost mystical respect for the spirit of 291 and its proprietor is documented in the pages of *Camera Work*, the gallery's quarterly magazine.

After the Armory Show, the number of galleries exhibiting modern American art increased rapidly. Of the older dealers, N. E. Montross was the first to be converted. Martin Birnbaum at the Berlin Photographic Gallery showed the work of Maurice Sterne and several others. Marius de Zayas, Charles Daniel, and Stephan Bourgeois all founded new galleries devoted to modern art; Daniel was particularly active and courageous in launching young and untried artists. In Brooklyn Hamilton Easter Field converted a room in one of his houses on the Heights into a gallery to show the work of his protégés. Henry Fitch Taylor, himself an abstract painter, directed the Madison Gallery in New York.

Another pressing problem for the modern artists was the lack of informed critics qualified to judge their work and explain it to the public. At the beginning most of the established figures, men like Arthur Hoeber, Royal Cortissoz, Frank Jewett Mather, Jr., were strongly opposed to all forms of modernism. A few, like James Huneker and Sadakichi Hartmann, tried harder to be fair but generally took their place with the opposition. One of the first to be converted

was Charles H. Caffin. In 1907 Caffin had finished writing his *Story of American Painting* with a rather pessimistic view of its future, but, as we have seen, his talk with Matisse two years later opened his eyes to the aims of the modern movement which he defended vigorously thereafter, even standing up for Alfred Maurer when few voices were raised in the latter's support.

Caffin was only one of a growing group of critics who were closely associated with Stieglitz and wrote extensively for *Camera Work*. Marius de Zayas, the Mexican born caricaturist, was another who was converted to modernism about 1911. With Paul B. Haviland, also of the Stieglitz group, he wrote an extended essay, *A Study of The Modern Evolution of Plastic Expression*, published by 291 in pamphlet form in 1913 — cloudy and obscure but perhaps the first general exposition of modern art to appear outside a magazine in this country. One of Stieglitz's most interesting contributors was John Weichsel, whose distrust of cubism's intellectual basis and whose argument for a universal abstract art based on "racial" plastic relations (by which he meant those rooted in the unchanging, primitive nature of man) were intelligently argued.

Outside the Stieglitz group several new critics with a genuine liking for modern art began to appear. Henry McBride on the *Sun* and Elisabeth Luther Cary on the *Times* wrote of the new art with warmth and understanding. Guy Pène du Bois in *Arts and Decoration*, W. D. MacColl and Willard Huntington Wright in *Forum* came to the defense of the Armory Show. Walter Pach did sympathetic articles for various magazines. Books on modern art began to appear. The first and in some ways the best, despite its rather confused organization, was Arthur Jerome Eddy's *Cubists and Post-Impressionism*, published in 1914. This was followed a year later by Willard Huntington Wright's *Modern Painting*, a more orderly discussion of the various movements but violently partisan to Synchromism, of which his brother Macdonald-Wright had been cofounder. (Later Wright followed his convictions to their logical conclusion when he argued that the art of the future lay in the color organ; thereafter he gave up art criticism and became a detective-story writer under the name of S. S. Van Dine.)

Finally, in *The Arts*, founded by Hamilton Easter Field in 1921 and long edited by Forbes Watson, we had our first independent and progressive art magazine.

In the meantime, American artists and their friends were doing what they could to win recognition for the new movements. This was little compared to what was accomplished abroad, for there were no closely organized groups here, with the possible exception of the Synchromists who followed the European pattern of manifestoes and well-publicized shows. For the most part it was a case of liberal artists combining and recombining in sporadic efforts to get modern art before the public. The Armory Show was the result of such an effort. So was the Forum Exhibition of 1916, assembled by a committee of progressive artists and critics including Henri, Stieglitz, Christian Brinton, Willard Huntington Wright, and several others. From fifty names submitted, the committee made its choice of the sixteen "best" modernists in America and gave them an impressive group show. On a smaller scale, the same thing was tried elsewhere. In Philadelphia Morton L. Schamberg assembled the first modern exhibition at the McClees Gallery, also in 1916. Various groups with common interests such as the Introspectives or the members of the Penguin, an informal anti-academic club, were also holding shows at about this time.

The most successfully sustained effort, however, was inspired by a principle rather than a community of interest. "No jury — no prizes," was at the heart of the Independent movement, whose goal was to establish an annual exhibition in which any artist, modern or academic, professional or amateur, could have his work hung by payment of a small entrance fee. The idea had been born in Paris with the founding of the Société des Artistes Indépendants in 1884, but the first attempts at an American equivalent were abortive. Of these we have already discussed the so-called "Original Independent Show" organized in 1908 by Arnold Friedman, Glenn O. Coleman, and Julius Golz. Friedman's account makes clear, however, that the contributors were more or less hand-picked and that even so "some were excluded." [6] The first truly nonjury exhibit appears to have been the one organized by members of the Eight with Kuhn, Bellows, du Bois, and others and

**127**

held in a loft building at 29 West 35th Street in 1910. "Over two thousand people attended the reception and nearly as many were turned away after the galleries were crowded to the limit of their capacity," it was reported. "A waiting line extended nearly to the end of the block, and finally police assistance was found necessary." [7] In spite of this success, the exhibition was not repeated.

Seven years passed before a permanent organization, the Society of Independent Artists, was finally formed in 1917 with William Glackens its first president and Charles Prendergast, Walter Pach, John R. Covert, and Walter Arensberg filling other offices. Its first exhibition, held in April at the Grand Central Palace, was a model of democratic fairness: the hanging was done in strictly alphabetical order; of some twenty-five hundred works submitted only one was rejected — Marcel Duchamp's Dadaist urinal, "La Fontaine." For many years thereafter, largely under the presidency of John Sloan, the Society held its huge spring annual, open to all who could pay its modest membership fee. While it was always well filled with the outlandish and incompetent, many good artists received their first recognition in its galleries. The idea spread elsewhere. Charles H. Walther organized the Society of Baltimore Independent Artists and Chicago started a series of Independent exhibitions in 1922. The same year saw the secession from the New York Society of a group, led by Field, which founded the Salons of America, thus giving the city a second nonjury annual. Later the movement dwindled as museums and other institutions liberalized their exhibition policies partially removing the need which it originally filled. Today most of the Independent groups are extinct or inactive, although sporadic efforts to revive them have been made. And it must be admitted that no juried or invited exhibition, no matter how liberal, can entirely replace the old free-for-all spirit of the Independents.

The support of modern art was only an incidental part of the Independent program; it was the main object of another group of artists who called themselves the Société Anonyme. Founded in 1920 by the abstract painter, Katherine S. Dreier, in collaboration with Marcel Duchamp and Man Ray, the Société launched an ambitious program of exhibitions and began forming its permanent collection for a museum of modern art, now at Yale University. In addition to the many group and one-man shows of modern European and American painters held in their New York gallery, the Société sent an incredible number of exhibitions to museums, schools, colleges, clubs, state fairs, and community centers throughout the country, spreading the knowledge of modern art in a way that had not been attempted before. Its collection was formed with great catholicity of taste and today it is the only public one in which the work of several of our obscure early modernists, such as Bruce and Covert, can be found.

These were some of the pioneering efforts which American artists themselves made to close the breach with the public. They were aided eventually by the country's museums, but the older of these were slow to overcome their conservative distrust of modernism. In 1913 Bryson Burroughs had persuaded the Metropolitan Museum to buy a Cézanne, the first to enter a public collection here, and in the same year the Newark Museum gave Weber a one-man show. But it was not until 1921 that modern art began to receive museum recognition on any scale. In that year there was a sudden outburst of exhibitions. The Worcester Art Museum showed a group of paintings assembled by the Société Anonyme; in New York the Brooklyn and Metropolitan Museums both held large exhibits of modern French art; in Philadelphia the Pennsylvania Academy of the Fine Arts gave American painters their chance in its "Later Tendencies" exhibition, reviewed in *The Arts* as "the best show of modern American art ever held." [8] Thereafter the established museums became gradually more liberal in their policies.

The most progressive work in this field was done, however, by a growing number of new museums founded by individuals who were interested in promoting creative art in America. In 1915 Mrs. Gertrude Vanderbilt Whitney helped found and support the Friends of the Young Artists, out of which grew, three years later, the Whitney Studio Club with Mrs. Juliana Force as its director. The club gave its artist members a series of group and one-man shows including an Overseas Exhibition which toured Europe in 1920–1921. By 1928 it had

**129**

six hundred members and three hundred applicants for whom there was no room. It was therefore transformed into the Whitney Studio Galleries and three years later into its final form, the Whitney Museum of American Art, as which it has continued to function as one of the most active and progressive forces in our art.

Actually the first museum devoted chiefly to work by living artists was the Phillips Gallery in Washington, D. C., founded by Duncan Phillips in 1918. With rare perception and independence, Phillips has given an unusual measure of support to those artists, like Dove and Knaths, in whom he has had special faith; in the end his judgments have usually been confirmed by critical opinion elsewhere. Five years later Albert C. Barnes established the Barnes Foundation in Merion, Pennsylvania, with his fine collection of modern French art, but its influence has been limited to the Foundation's students as its founder has rigorously excluded the public.

While it came too late to play a part in the early struggle, the Museum of Modern Art in New York, founded in 1929, has probably done more than any other single institution to educate the public in the aims and methods of the contemporary artist. Under the guidance of Alfred H. Barr, Jr., it has produced a series of exhibitions and monographs tracing the various modern movements, uncovering new talent both here and abroad, and reporting developments in architecture, photography, industrial design, and other relatively neglected arts. Its unusual combination of scholarship and showmanship has given it an influential position in its field. More specialized, the Solomon R. Guggenheim Foundation's Museum of Non-Objective Painting, founded in 1937, has given abstract art its own exclusive temple. Outside New York many other museums, societies, and institutes devoted to modern art have sprung up while nearly all the older museums now give it a larger place than before in their exhibitions and purchases.

In spite of these many activities in his support, the modern artist, with some exceptions, has fared rather poorly in the important matter of making enough money to live. In the early years of the century the large collectors of modern art could be numbered on one's fingers. Some, like the Steins, were extraordinarily generous and did much to help the painters in whom they were interested through the perennial crises which beset the world's most uncertain occupation. Without the support of Mrs. Nathan J. Miller, Weber could scarcely have continued to paint. John Quinn and Lizzie Bliss in New York, Duncan Phillips in Washington, Ferdinand Howald in Ohio, Etta and Claribel Cone in Baltimore, Walter C. Arensberg in New York and California — these, and several others in a more modest way, built early collections which helped the pioneers of the modern movements at a time when help was most needed.

Yet even their devoted efforts were small compared with the need. In the nineteenth century the artist had had a second string to his bow in illustrating, which was then not so far removed aesthetically from his more serious interests. The paintings and the illustrations which Homer did of Civil War subjects are essentially in the same vein, and as late as the time of the Eight magazine work required no surrender of aesthetic standards, only perhaps a lesser effort. Even comic strips, as Luks and Feininger demonstrated, could be infused with many of the qualities of their authors' paintings. For the abstract artist and the expressionist, however, this adjustment became virtually impossible. Even for the more realistic painters it was difficult, since magazine illustrations evolved in the direction of a slick impressionism with which it was hard to compete on more sober terms. Caricature remained one of the few commercial outlets for the creative artist, as Gropper's cartoons and the drawings of the *New Yorker* group witnessed, but this was a small field which could not contain many. The attempt of the newspaper *PM* to revive pictorial reporting in the 1940's was not very successful, and while artist correspondents during the second World War did some excellent work, the photographers on the whole did better.

As a result, the career of nearly every modern artist without independent means has been studded with excursions into other occupations. Burchfield and Hopper for many years gave up their serious painting entirely and did commercial work. Sheeler and Kuniyoshi

**131**

became photographers. Others ran elevators, restaurants, beauty shops, worked in factories, shipyards, on ranches and farms. Hundreds taught art in private classes or the various schools. All of them suffered to some extent, many tragically, from the drain of energy and the enforced estrangement from their work.

Then came the wasting economic depression of the 1930's and with it this country's only large-scale experiment in government sponsorship of the arts. Perhaps because of our tendency to regard art as an easily dispensible luxury, American painters were among the first to feel the dire effects of curtailed spending, nor was there any official agency in the government to which they could look for relief. For we were then and are now once more one of the few civilized nations of the world without a federal bureau devoted to the support and encouragement of the fine arts. A century and a half of efforts to correct this omission have so far been unsuccessful in spite of the constructive results which the temporary measures of the depression produced.

The first of these measures was the establishment in 1933 of the Public Works of Art Project, administered by Edward Bruce and Forbes Watson under the Treasury Department. The country was divided into sixteen regions with a volunteer committee in charge of each, and no one did a more difficult or devoted job than the members of these committees in screening the flood of desperate applications which descended on them. In June 1934 this project had to be abandoned and for a time there were only small state projects operating under the Federal Emergency Relief Administration. But in August 1935 these were all absorbed in the most comprehensive effort of all, the Federal Art Project of the Works Progress Administration. To supervise this, Harry Hopkins called Holger Cahill to Washington. Regional directors were appointed, and in each region state and local divisions were set up. The arts were classified in some fifteen categories: mural painting, easel painting, graphic arts, sculpture, and so forth; several unusual projects were also undertaken, such as the Index of American Design, a series of wonderfully precise drawings of early American furniture, textiles, and other crafts. Under Cahill's liberal and understanding direction the painters and sculptors were permitted to work in their own studios, on their own subjects, in their own styles.

Those opposed to government sponsorship of the arts have pointed to the fairly large body of mediocre work which the Project did indeed produce. They forget that this was primarily a relief measure and that human need took precedence over high aesthetic standards. Even had it been otherwise, this would have been a small price to pay for what the Project accomplished. Some of our best and most famous artists, men like Stuart Davis, Yasuo Kuniyoshi, and Marsden Hartley, could not have continued without its aid. Great numbers of our promising younger artists — Levine, Breinin, Graves, Bloom, MacIver, and scores of others — whose careers were just starting in the early 1930's, might well have been forced to give up painting without its encouragement. To many of these the Project gave their first opportunity to work full time at their art. The loss to the creative forces in American life which was averted by the Federal Art Project and the allied program of the Treasury Department's Section of Fine Arts would indeed have been a serious one.

The moral has been, unfortunately, less apparent to our legislators than to others. Since the final dissolution of the Project in 1943, several attempts by government agencies to make use of American art have failed in almost every instance to win Congressional approval. Appropriations for the War Department's plan to send painters to the various theaters in the last war were eliminated by Congress in 1943 and, as we shall see later, pressure was placed on the State Department to withdraw its traveling exhibition of modern pictures. Within very recent years, the American Federation of Arts and several other independent bodies have renewed the attempt to establish a government bureau of art with a long-range plan for its encouragement and wider dissemination through the country. Sooner or later such a step seems inevitable, but whether it can be accomplished in the near future is still difficult to judge.

Several other new avenues have opened to the artist in the last twenty years or so, which have promised much, although in many cases the promise has proved ephemeral. Chief of these is the patronage of the creative artist by American industries without the usual demand that his work be commercialized to meet the low standards of slick-paper advertisements. The water colors which Marsh and others have done for the Standard Oil Company, or the semi-abstract designs of de Kooning, Charles Howard, and Man Ray for the Container Corporation are cases in point. The annual exhibitions of Pepsi-Cola, from which the subjects for their calendars were drawn, the advertisements of Abbott Laboratories and Lucky Strike, the extensive though rather conservative collection of International Business Machines are other variations on a trend, if we can call it that, toward more adult standards in commercial art. Unfortunately many of these efforts have been discontinued, and it is difficult to tell whether they are the genuine portents of a movement that may draw the artist into closer relation with our material civilization or whether they are only a brief and experimental flowering.

Like industry, labor too has solicited the help of the artist. Its patronage has not yet been as extensive as that of the large corporations but the cartoons of Gropper, the brilliant posters which Shahn has done for the Political Action Committee of the CIO, and the illustrated booklets of the Maritime Union and perhaps others appear to be the harbingers of a spreading use of art for propaganda and instruction. Regardless of one's political convictions, one cannot deny that the unions have forged some extraordinarily sharp pictorial weapons by employing creative artists sympathetic to their cause.

What, then, is the modern artist's material position today? Museums have multiplied in the twentieth century and more contemporary art is purchased for public collections than at any time in our history. Industry and labor have become patrons, at least tentatively. Commercial galleries exhibiting modern art have increased manyfold and even department stores have entered this field, though seldom for long. The buying public has widened greatly; no longer can one point to a few devoted collectors of ample means; to their number have been added thousands of small collectors whose total purchases may exceed those of the wealthy.

Yet these gains are more apparent than real, for the last half century has also seen an even greater increase in the number of artists. In 1902 Sadakichi Hartmann estimated that this had "increased to an alarming extent. There are about three thousand artists in New York, Boston and Philadelphia alone." [9] The 1940 census listed 13,897 for the same three cities and this figure was not complete. Statistics are unreliable, but it seems evident that this increase represents an enrichment of our art at the expense of the individual artist. Such a conclusion is supported by the results of a poll conducted by Elizabeth McCausland in 1946.[10] Questionnaires were sent to five hundred of America's most prominent artists, chosen on the basis of the frequency with which they exhibited in the various large annual shows. About forty per cent replied. Of these the average yearly income from all sources was $4,144, but the average from sale of their art (commercial work excluded) was only $1,154. And this, it must be emphasized, was no random cross section of our painters and sculptors but a hand-picked list of our presumably most successful men.

While they have long been painfully aware of this condition, it is only recently that the artists, themselves, have taken concerted action to improve it. Artists Equity Association, founded in 1947, is the first "national, non-political, esthetically non-partisan organization" aiming purely at the economic betterment of its members that we have had in this country. Its ambitious program would not only establish legal protection from various forms of exploitation, but would also take practical steps to promote the use and diffusion of art throughout the country. It has made an auspicious start, although it is still too soon to tell how effective it will be.

## 11

## TRENDS AND PORTENTS

It is apparent that modern art in America, despite its constantly growing strength, has not yet won its battle for a recognition wide enough to nourish and support it in its quest for the complex truths of our time. The breach that became apparent at the Armory Show was perhaps most successfully bridged during the late twenties and the decade of the thirties when many of our artists paused to digest the lessons of abstract art and expressionism and a large public nearly caught up with them. Now that they have reëntered the vanguard of experiment and new creation, the breach has again widened, at least momentarily.

This does not mean that we have returned to the conditions of 1913, for the nature of the schism has changed considerably in the course of the years. Materialism and indifference to art are still with us, but insofar as such things can be measured they seem to have diminished. Nor are we, as a people, so closely bound to strict realism in our aesthetic beliefs. Abstract design when wedded to recognizable subject matter, as in the work of the Immaculates, or to function, as in our industrial and decorative arts, is generally acceptable. Pure abstraction is not; it is still offensive and bewildering to many and its wide revival in recent years is the largest cause of popular animosity. It has not, however, been the only one. As we have seen, much genuinely creative work continues to be done outside the abstract movement. Here ideological differences of opinion are often present, for the representational painting of our time has concerned itself increasingly with the problems of man in our complex and fearful civilization. The doubts which surrealism has cast on the rational powers of humanity and the doubts which the socially conscious painters have expressed on the justice of our socio-political ways have aroused the bitter enmity of those who would confine all philosophical or sociological thought to safely worn channels. Paradoxically, the chief opposition to modern art today is based partly on the abstract painter's so-called divorce of art and life, partly on the realist's too deep concern with life's controversial issues.

The reactionary counterattack in the 1940's has taken place on two levels of intelligence. An instance of the lowest type of prejudiced and uninformed criticism was provided by the Hearst press in its campaign against the State Department's traveling exhibition of modern American art. In 1946 the Department, in answer to requests from abroad, had purchased seventy-nine paintings representing the more advanced movements. These were exhibited first at the Metropolitan Museum in New York where they were fairly and in general favorably reviewed by the professional critics of the city's press. They were then sent abroad on a projected tour of various countries and were actually exhibited in Haiti, Paris, and Prague, where they seem to have been warmly received and aroused much interest. Their tour was cut short in 1947, however, when the Hearst press, with certain conservative art organizations, embarked on a campaign of ridicule and vilification which made no attempt to understand the aims or methods of modern art, but took advantage of the uninformed public's natural bewilderment by reassuring them that only common sense was needed to see that this art was ugly, absurd, junk, lunatic delight, and the like. Acutely sensitive to charges of extravagance and un-Americanism, several members of Congress whose knowledge of art was questionable added their voices to the protest while the President made a caustic reference to one of the pictures. Under this pressure, the exhibition was canceled and the paintings were turned over to the War Assets Administration, which sold them in 1948 for a fraction of their original cost — not because they were worthless, as some reports of the sale implied, but because all except five of the pictures were allotted, under the Administration's system of priorities, to public institutions which received a ninety-five per cent discount.

Often, in these days of political tension, criticism of this kind resorts to the epithet "communistic," which it tends to apply indiscriminately to all art which it dislikes. As far as abstract painting is concerned, the appellation is patently absurd, for the highly regimented arts of Soviet Russia are uniformly naturalistic and abstraction is a form of "bourgeois aestheticism" which is not permitted. There may be, among our painters of social comment, members of the American Communist Party. In relation to our modern art as a whole, their number would seem to be infinitesimal and their paintings, as far as I am aware, have never preached forcible overthrow of our democratic government. Their central theme has been social injustice and those undemocratic flaws in our country which most liberal Americans deplore. As such, their work can scarcely be branded "communistic," even if their personal sympathies should lie in that direction. To attempt to discredit all modern painting through a loose and inaccurate stigmatization of one of its smallest parts is characteristic of the biased and emotional nature of the reactionary counterattack at its most irresponsible.

We cannot so lightly dismiss, however, the objections of intelligent critics and scholars who do not like modernism, especially abstraction, for a variety of reasons which have some basis in fact. Their arguments against the validity of abstract expression may be collectively summarized as follows: first, that it is a form of escapism which refuses to deal with the experiences and problems of life; second, that it is exclusively self-expressionist, an art of private symbols and forms which fails to communicate with the average spectator; third, that it is un-American, not in a chauvinistic sense but in depending too heavily on unassimilated foreign influences, such as that of Picasso; fourth, that much of it lacks craftsmanship and is a refuge for the incompetent. Those who do not make the first charge often add a fifth: that it is a too faithful reflection of the sterile scientific determinism and empty morality which they believe to be characteristic of our times.

These are serious objections and there is an element of truth in several of them, although I believe it is only a partial truth which is qualified or controverted by other considerations. We must examine these objections carefully, for they are advanced in good faith by men of knowledge and integrity.

Is abstract art a form of escapism? One of its staunchest defenders, Lloyd Goodrich, has written: "The prevalence of abstract art in the periods of the two World Wars may have still another significance. Abstraction may serve as an escape from troubling realities into a world of aesthetic order where the artist is in full control, just as surrealism is an escape into the world of private fantasy." [1] But is this actually escape? It might be more precise to say that the artist who works with the classical forms of abstraction is attempting to establish order out of chaos, to build new values in a troubled world, to reaffirm the dignity of man as a rational creature; that the surrealist is struggling to reaffirm the mysterious intuitive powers of man's spirit. These answers cannot be accepted by those who hold that the artist only mirrors the *Zeitgeist*, or spirit of the times. But for those who believe that he is sometimes more instrumental than other men in creating the *Zeitgeist* of the future, this "escape" from the present can well be viewed as a constructive effort in that direction.

The charge of escapism, however, is advanced in still another sense which holds that the abstract artist has deliberately refused to deal with common experience, that he has dehumanized his art by banishing subject matter, has impoverished it of all the associative and literary values which have enriched Western painting since the Renaissance and made it into a coldly scientific and intellectual exercise. If this charge is qualified to apply only to that relatively small body of art which is totally abstract in the classical line of the movement, its truth must be admitted. Art of this kind is narrow, but it is also deep. It has sacrificed associative values to try to speak the language of pure form, and, as Emerson remarked, "It is a proof of the shallowness of the doctrine of beauty as it lies in the minds of our amateurs, that men seem to have lost the perception of the instant dependence of form upon soul." [2] It is intellectual but not cold, for intelligence generates its own passion. It is a rather special kind of art which will probably never appeal to a great many people, but there have been other special kinds of art in the past which are no less genuine because of their self-imposed

**139**

limitations. At the opposite pole from pure abstraction, for instance, there is the work of the extreme realists in the nineteenth century. Considering them, in 1883, Charles Larned exclaimed, "Intellect has broken jail and stalks abroad, armed with the scalpel and the lens, while the heart carefully dissected hangs at its girdle," [3] words strangely prophetic of a kind of criticism now frequently leveled at abstraction.

The second charge, that abstract art fails to communicate with the average spectator, is certainly true today. But we must ask whether the failure is the artist's and, if true today, whether it will be so tomorrow? For at least the last hundred years, new art movements have often proved unintelligible to the general audience of their time but have been widely understood and appreciated by succeeding generations. The artist's responsibility is not to the common denominator of public intelligence but to the highest, from which his meaning will spread in time to wider understanding. He cannot be required to popularize his thought any more than the scientist or the mathematician, for all seek truth, and truth, in its newly discovered aspects, is often difficult to comprehend. This is widely recognized by the more intelligent opponents of modern art, and yet they feel that abstract painters, particularly those in the surrealist line, are somehow an exception, that their art is so entirely personal and introspective, so deeply obscured by unexplained private symbols, that it can never be fully comprehensible to anyone but the artists themselves. This is an oblique recognition of the fact that art of this kind is purposely irrational, hallucinatory, fantastic, and dreamlike; insofar as it makes use of automatism, we may even doubt whether it is entirely clear to the artist himself. It is illogical, then, to expect that it will ever be fully explicable in rational terms. But if it awakens echoes of strangeness in the spectator and stimulates his imagination with suggestions of elusive meanings and emotions, it will have *communicated* as forcibly in its own way as the more explicit forms of a rational art. This it does, indeed, to those who are willing to meet it on its own ground.

Another hindrance to communication is the inescapable fact that we no longer have, as in the past, a single, homogeneous style easily understood by all; since the middle of the nineteenth century new movement has followed new movement with bewildering diversity and speed. As René d'Harnoncourt has demonstrated, this diversity has been the result of the growth of personal freedoms and of a corresponding individualism. "Freed from the restriction of collective style, the artist discovered he could create a style in the image of his own personality. The art of the twentieth century has no collective style, not because it has divorced itself from contemporary society but because it is part of it." If, then, our object in a democracy is to create "an order which reconciles the freedom of the individual with the welfare of society . . . we must welcome its equivalent in the arts. To expect a diversified society to produce a uniform, universally understood art is a measure of our true fear of facing the results of our own advances." [4]

The third charge, that abstract art is un-American in the sense of having no roots in our soil and depending too heavily on European models, raises problems which we shall discuss later. For the moment we may point out that our art has always been a part of the larger Western tradition, from which it would be as impossible for us to divorce ourselves as it would be to turn our civilization into an Oriental one. The revolutionary advance in communications during the last century has inevitably lessened our material and spiritual isolation and involved us in international movements of which art is but one. Even so, much of our abstract painting is more supra- than inter-national, as Robert Motherwell has pointed out; while another large part of it is still deeply colored with local and national feeling, as the work of Marin, Dove, Stuart Davis, and others can testify. Both kinds seem equally valid, for they draw on creative thought and emotion though they find them in different sources. The empty copyist, who apes Picasso without feeling or understanding, exists in numbers and is deplorable. But his counterpart has existed in every period and is no more or less deplorable when he apes Benton or Marsh or Curry in the same way.

The objection that abstract art lacks craftsmanship and is a refuge for the incompetent is seldom seriously advanced, for several of our abstract and semi-abstract painters have demonstrated their ability to draw or paint with a precise realism which would be the despair of

**141**

many academicians. Sheeler's work is a case in point. Moreover, abstraction itself often requires great technical skill, as the dexterous experiments of Rice Pereira with glass, plastics, parchment, and various new media have shown. It is sometimes harder to detect incompetence in abstract than in representational art, and it is doubtless true that many a young painter with imperfect technical equipment has been tempted to hide his shortcomings in cubes and cones, but sooner or later these become painfully apparent, as anyone who has looked at much student work can testify.

The most serious charge of all is the last one: that modern art reflects our faithless, iconoclastic world with its sterile scientific determinism. This is the reverse of the charge of escapism, for it maintains that the artist is no more responsible for our spiritual poverty than any other man, that his art inevitably reflects conditions as they are and may therefore be a valuable social document, but is none the less decadent. Those who hold this view can point with some justice to the mockery of Dada, to the savage phases of Picasso's art, to the large body of morbid work which surrealism has unquestionably produced. In the representational field, they can point to Cadmus or Koerner as mirrors of decadence or to certain pictures by Kuniyoshi and Evergood as reflections of despair.

This is obviously too sweeping an indictment when applied to al' modern art, for it ignores the many shades of feeling within the work of every movement and artist. It overlooks the fact that if Picasso has been savage, he has also been gentle and full of lyric poetry, that if surrealism has been sensational, it has also helped to define the nature of man's intuitive powers, that if cubism and the other classical phases of abstraction have been revolutionary, they have been so only in their extreme emphasis on the Platonic virtues of order, clarity, and reason. In American art it disregards the large body of work which falls so plainly outside its strictures. No one can well mistake the ample and courageous strength of Marin, Hartley, Dove, Hopper, Sheeler, Feininger, and a good many more of our leading figures. Theirs is an art of spiritual affirmation which transcends despair and finds its inspiration in the dignity of man and the beauty of nature. Still others, like

Weber and Franklin Watkins, have of course dealt directly with religious themes in a spirit of genuine reverence.

But such criticisms are sins of omission, albeit important, and the larger indictment deserves a more direct answer. No one can deny that much modern art is indeed touched with pessimism and bitterness, but the important point is that these qualities are not necessarily deplorable and that, above all, they are not synonymous with decadence or materialism. The tragic sense of life has informed some of the greatest art of the Western world from the time of Greek civilization to the present. Art of this kind is as firmly rooted in spiritual values as that which celebrates man's lot in a more optimistic vein; indeed it is perhaps more deeply concerned with such values because of its despair at their submersion or violation.

Our own painting of the last fifty years would be poorer without the bitterness and irony of Shahn, Evergood, Levine, and many others, because they distilled a gall of protest, not of resignation, and thus affirmed their faith in man. The gray despair of Kuniyoshi's wartime pictures was the direct reaction of a sensitive painter to a spiritual catastrophe. The preoccupation with mortal transience and decay, which a few of our artists like Albright and Hyman Bloom have shown, is the somber but not the hopeless side of a metaphysical concern with ultimate reality. The strange symbols of Graves, Stamos, Gottlieb, and others are the still plainer instruments of a search for spiritual values. In contrast to these men, our true apostles of materialism do not appear to be the modernists, but those academic or commercial painters whose fleshly nudes and edible still lifes speak to the senses alone. Some of our romantic realists have moved dangerously close to this position, but few have succumbed.

*Zeitgeist* is always a dangerous generalization. The charge that modern art or abstraction or surrealism is a mirror of decadence is generally an a priori argument which first establishes its pessimistic view of our civilization and then relates an art which it dislikes and misunderstands to the unhappy state of the world. Even a historian like Arnold Toynbee, who finds enough spiritual strength in our society to be cautiously optimistic, can see in modern art nothing but the break-

**143**

down of spiritual values. And this for no demonstrable reason except that our art has parted, in his opinion, with Western tradition and that some of it has drawn new life from primitive sources. It might be more just to conclude that modern art is a language which such critics have learned to read imperfectly.

We have tried to answer some of the commonest objections to modern art, but the only real answer is the astonishing variety and vitality of that art itself. From neglect, abuse, and literal starvation, the modern artist has fought a long and discouragingly slow battle toward a more general recognition which is yet far from complete. The true strength of the movement is finally becoming apparent, however. Its growing acceptance in exhibitions, in public collections, and in contemporary criticism has already been noted. In addition, it has begun to spread through our general educational system as one of today's humanities. Some of our older universities with long-established art galleries excluded it until recently. Now modern collections will be found at Harvard and Yale and at a great many others, while in the west several state universities, notably those of Nebraska, Illinois, and Iowa, have instituted annual or biennial exhibitions of contemporary work from which they purchase regularly. The artist-in-residence has become a fixture in many smaller colleges, and some of our leading modern painters and sculptors have filled such positions. The American Federation of Arts, once extremely conservative, now circulates exhibitions of modern art throughout the country, while the College Art Association takes an active part in its discussion and teaching. The list could be extended for several pages.

In the face of such evidence, it is apparent that the modern movements can no longer be dismissed as a cult or a fashion. It was never very perceptive to do so, but at least there was greater excuse for the bewildered critics of 1913 than for those of today. Modern art has won the hardest part of its battle; it must still find a way to touch the lives of more of our people, and time is apparently helping it to do this.

Meanwhile it is not, of course, standing still but is constantly developing, changing, experimenting. At the moment abstract and semi-abstract art is in the ascendancy, but it would be a brave critic who would dare predict what the future balance between these and the representational modes of painting will be. Some feel that a slackening in the abstract tide is already noticeable and that we may likely enter a period of pause and consolidation similar to that of the 1920's. Others believe passionately that any return toward naturalism is a retreat and a betrayal; that the only possible future for American art lies in abstraction and expressionism.

Perhaps the question is not so important as it would seem to be, for there are many degrees of abstraction between extreme realism and the totally abstract; most of our painters work somewhere in this middle ground and whether they are nearer one end of the scale than the other is perhaps less significant than what they have to say. One might, for instance, link Hopper, Feininger, and Marin, in spite of their great stylistic differences, because all three are so intimately concerned with the moods of nature, as they have shown in their paintings and explicitly stated in their writings.* This is only a partial truth, of course, for form does modify content and the shifting aesthetic standards between naturalism and abstraction are important to the communication of the artist's emotion.

The quality of that emotion is also a variable factor which cuts across style, and here we may perhaps see a well-defined trend. At one extreme is the classical artist who conceives the world in terms of rational relationships and finds beauty in a precise intellectual order, at the other the romantic artist whose values are those of intuition and feeling, of mystery, suggestion, and a more obvious emotionalism. Discussing the course of abstract art, Alfred Barr noted in 1935 that while the classical line had predominated at the beginning, it had by then

---

*"My aim in painting," wrote Hopper in the catalogue of his exhibition at the Museum of Modern Art in 1933, "has always been the most exact transcription possible of my most intimate impressions of nature." "You have to follow them [nature's laws]" said Marin, "just as nature follows them" (Dorothy Norman, "Marin Speaks . . . and Stieglitz," *Magazine of Art*, 30:151, 1937). Others might excel in color, Feininger admitted in a letter of 1917, "But the feeling for nature, which *I* own seems to me very wonderful also, and perhaps leading into greater depths . . ." (Museum of Modern Art, Feininger-Hartley Exhibition, 1944, Catalogue, p. 18).

**145**

been largely submerged in the romantic one.[5] Today, as we have previously shown, the trend toward romantic forms of abstraction has become even more pronounced, particularly among the younger men who will determine the future directions of our art. If this is true of the abstract movement, it is no less so in the representational field. Expressionism, which is still one of the major currents in American painting, is predominantly romantic; of the various kinds of realism, it is romantic realism which has the largest following, although extreme realism has recently shown signs of greater vitality. This does not mean that classical forms are entirely absent from our art. There is still a vigorous classical minority among our painters and sculptors, while in modern architecture the International Style continues to dominate the others. Nevertheless classicism appears to be momentarily waning, and it seems likely that, in the near future at least, our art will follow a generally romantic direction.

Within this wide classification there will probably be for many years as much diversity of movements and individual styles as there is today. Yet it may also be that we are now in a transitional period from which a dominant movement will in time emerge. "In periods of transition," wrote S. R. Koehler in 1880, "in which some men adhere to old faiths, and others tear themselves away from them while the new faith that is to be their light is still hidden from all, or at best but dimly seen . . . individualism asserts itself . . . there being no generally recognized leaders."[6] With the advantage of hindsight, it is now easy enough to see what was happening to American art in 1880 as the sharply focused realism of the mid-century yielded to various strains of impressionism. Looking back at the 1940's a half century hence, it may be possible to say that in these years the foundation was laid for the ultimate triumph of abstraction, of expressionism, of some kind of realism, or even, conceivably, of a mystical and visionary art. Today all these movements have so much vitality that it is difficult to believe any is on the verge of extinction, and it is equally possible, as René d'Harnoncourt has pointed out, that diversity and change are now permanent characteristics of our art.[7]

In a recent symposium on "The State of American Art" a group of critics was asked, among others, two questions: "Is there a well-marked trend or direction of style in American painting and sculpture today?" and "How does it appear to you that American art today . . . stacks up against the Old World in quality of individual accomplishment and vigor of general activity?" [8] With a few exceptions the answers were remarkably similar: that no single dominant trend could be perceived, but that American art in its vitality and originality compared very well indeed with that of any European country, if the work of the great pioneer modernists abroad, who still survive from an earlier generation, be excepted.

# 12

## WHAT IS AMERICAN?

Throughout our history, the relation of American art to that of Europe has been a subject of controversy. Have we a genuine native art with recognizable characteristics, or have we only a provincial reflection of foreign movements? If our art is national, what makes it so? If it is not, can it be international? What is the effect of foreign study, of expatriation, of close indentification with European-born movements? These are some of the questions which have risen in the past and which continue to divide critics and artists today.

There is, by now, fairly general agreement that we have indeed produced a native art which is more than a pale imitation of European models, though plainly an integral part of the European tradition. There is no such agreement as to when our art first took on a pronounced native cast, some finding it in our earliest seventeenth-century work, some in the paintings of Copley, Peale, and other eighteenth-century figures, some claiming that the Hudson River School in the nineteenth century was our first native movement and a few, like Jerome Mellquist, believing that American art emerged fully from European bondage only in the twentieth century.[1] This seems, however, the least important consideration, for the truth is that a certain native flavor has appeared in much of our art since very nearly the beginning and it is only a question of when it became sufficiently pronounced to be recognized as the mark of an American School.

A more serious difference of opinion has been caused by attempts to find a single definition for this native flavor. Most efforts in this direction have followed the line laid down by an anonymous writer in

148

1815 who found that American painters were generally skilled "in acuteness of observation, in truth and accuracy," and were "chiefly deficient in cultivated taste, in variety and grace, and in generality and grandeur of conception." [2] With a prouder emphasis on the positive qualities, this opinion is echoed through the nineteenth century and well into the twentieth. "Now it is a curious thing," said Birge Harrison in 1909, "that, while we in America have for the past twenty years been discussing the question of whether any such thing as a national school of art exists here, in Paris '*l'Ecole Americaine*' has for fully as long a time been recognized as a distinct school . . . whose chief characteristic was an unusual directness and clarity of vision, coupled with a corresponding simplicity of statement." [3] A variation of this opinion, which placed greater stress on American subject matter and regional forms, was the central philosophy of the American Scene painters in the 1930's. Still another variation has recently been advanced by John A. Kouwenhoven, who finds the essence of American art in the simplicity and functionalism of our native crafts and in those paintings which he feels reflect the same "vernacular" tradition. [4]

Insofar as one can generalize, then, the commonest attempts to isolate the American quality in our art have centered on such adjectives as simple, naïve, vigorous, matter-of-fact, ingenious, realistic, independent, and the like, which are supposedly descriptive, too, of a common element in our national character. Of our nineteenth-century painters Homer is the prototype, in the twentieth it is Bellows, Benton, Curry, or Wood. But while such adjectives do indeed indicate a quality in many of our people and in much of our art, it is also obvious that they are totally inadequate for all of either. When the anonymous writer of 1815 was commenting on our artists' truth and accuracy and lack of variety and grace, Washington Allston was the foremost American painter, and it is hardly necessary to point out that his art is the exact opposite of those traits. Moreover Allston, while an isolated figure among our painters, was not unrepresentative of a fairly broad phase of American culture; his dreamy and visionary art, as E. P. Richardson has shown, was closely related to the "quietism" of Hawthorne's early stories and Longfellow's *Hyperion* and *Voices of the Night*, and to the

**149**

idealism of the Transcendentalists.[5] A theory which ignores so important an exception cannot lay claim to more than partial truth, and there has been no time since 1815 when equally important exceptions did not exist. The fantasy of Quidor and the seriousness of William Page, the brilliance of Homer and the darkness of Ryder, the idyls of Davies, and the dynamism of Stella are all coeval products of opposed phases of American civilization at various times. They are sharply native, but in different ways, and no single definition can embrace them all, for there is no common denominator apparent. The American character, in people or in art, is nonexistent in a monolithic sense, which is also true of any modern country today. We can only say that a variety of traits, often dissimilar and often changing, have been characteristic of some of our people and some of our art in the periods when they were dominant.

Those who seek a unifying spirit in American art are generally inspired by a prior conviction that our art *should* be wholly indigenous and that its virtue increases in proportion to its American-ness. Their definitions are often accompanied by animadversions against European art and those Americans who have come largely under its influence. Our expatriate artists have been a frequent target; they "do not, as a rule, compare in genuine manly results with those who are working right among us," a nineteenth-century sentiment echoed by Sadakichi Hartmann when he wrote, "Anybody who has a serious interest in the welfare of American art can feel but little sympathy for these Franco and Teuto-Americans, however one may admire their work." Kouwenhoven's dismay at the inroads which the sophisticated European tradition made on the "vernacular" and Craven's denunciation of "the emasculated tradition of the French modernists" and those American "intellectuals who tell us that art is an international business" are part of the same pattern.[6]

Since at least the middle of the nineteenth century, however, a vocal minority has pleaded for a greater rather than a lesser European influence on the theory that we are all part of a long Western tradition, that we can still learn much from Europe, and that our art will inevitably reflect American characteristics without self-consciously striving for them. This view was never more persuasively stated than by the brilliant American critic James Jackson Jarves, who wrote in 1864 that "if America elects to develop her art wholly out of herself, without reference to the accumulated experience of older civilizations, she will make a mistake, and protract her improvement. There is a set of men among us," Jarves continued, "who talk loftily of the independent, indigenous growth of American art; of its freedom of obligation to the rest of the world; of its inborn capacity to originate, invent, create, and make anew; of the spoiling of those minds whose instincts prompt them to study art where it is best understood and most worthily followed. Perhaps so! Nevertheless it would be a great waste of time to adopt such a system, and possibly it might fail. . . We have not time to invent and study everything anew. . . No one dreams of it in science, ethics, or physics. Why then propose it in art? We are a composite people. Our knowledge is eclectic. . . It remains, then, for us to be as eclectic in our art as in the rest of our civilization. To get artistic riches by virtue of assimilated examples, knowledge, and ideas, drawn from all sources, and made national and homogeneous by a solidarity of our own, is our right pathway to consummate art." [7]

It will be noted that Jarves did not argue against a native art but assumed that American painters would inevitably reflect American life. If that life had solidarity, then our art would be homogeneous; and, by implication, if that life was diversified, then our art would show diversity. In either case it would be as truly American as that which fell within the narrower limits of chauvinistic definitions.

In periods when extreme nationalism has waned, Jarves' position has been maintained by many others.

"Do you consider it right to give up your country?" one of James's characters asks the expatriate American in *Portrait of a Lady*.

"Ah, one doesn't give up one's country any more than one gives up one's grandmother," replies Ralph Touchett. "It's antecedent to choice."

"I have noted a tendency," said Robert Henri a good many years later, "to consider the paintings of a man who has never been abroad more American than those of a man who has been abroad. May as well

**151**

say that Benjamin Franklin left his American spirit in Philadelphia when he went to Europe." [8]

The evidence of our past art lends greater support to this theory than to that of the isolationists. Throughout the nineteenth century large numbers of our painters and sculptors studied and lived for long periods abroad. One thinks, at random, of Allston, Whittredge, Cropsey, G. L. Brown, Eastman Johnson, Duveneck, Theodore Robinson as well as the more famous expatriates such as Whistler, Sargent, and Cassatt. In their own day the European influences which they felt seemed, at times, the dominant elements in their work; Johnson was the "American Rembrandt," Brown the "American Claude." Today, these influences are less apparent, and few would deny that the paintings of this group have on the whole a marked native character — not because they share any single trait, but because they reflect various aspects of American life. If we can apply the lesson of history to our modern art, it would seem likely that even those men who now follow European models most closely may in time appear nearly as American as those who work more obviously in a native tradition.

Nearly, but not quite, for this theory also needs qualification. The expatriate artist may never be able to shed his American background, but he can and often does submerge it to a varying extent in the culture of another country or in an internationalism or supranationalism compounded of many elements. No one would claim that Whistler is as characteristically American as Homer or that the work which Eastman Johnson did in the Hague reflects American life as purely as his later paintings on Nantucket. Marin and Stuart Davis will without doubt always seem more native than Gorky or Morgan Russell. Perhaps we may say that the American quality in a work of art depends on two factors: the length of time that the artist has been exposed to an American environment and the artist's sensitivity to that environment.

This does not mean, of course, that the only native art is that which is concerned with American landscape, peoples, customs, and the like. Paradoxically, internationalism is as characteristic of American thought at certain times and places as is a more obvious nationalism. The former has manifested itself particularly during periods of upheaval such as

those of the two World Wars, and it is probably no accident, as Lloyd
Goodrich has pointed out, that the international style of abstract art
has had its greatest flowering in America during the years following
those conflicts.[9] Internationalism has also been stronger, at all times, in
the cities of the eastern seaboard than it has in the middle west; again it
is no accident that the apostles of the American scene were active in
the latter region while abstract art has centered in the former.

The ideological struggle between the two concepts of what
American art should be is influenced partly, therefore, by the waxing
and waning of a nationalistic spirit in the country as a whole, partly by
the perennial urban versus rural and eastern versus western split in
American life. One would enrich our national culture from all assimi-
lable sources, a process which logically leads towards internationalism,
though it does not at all preclude the persistence of native forms and
spirit. The other would enrich our culture by isolation and "purifica-
tion," strengthening those traits which it conceives to be indigenous
and rigorously excluding others. Its greatest theoretical weakness lies in
the impossibility of reaching any acceptable agreement on what these
indigenous characteristics are; its greatest practical weakness in the
impoverishment and eventual sterility which it would wreak on our art.

Probably there is no real choice involved, for the evolutionary
process appears to be slowly strengthening the urban, international
position, although there may be many fluctuations before it is generally
accepted. Nor is this necessarily deplorable, for the key to its validity
lies in the ability of the artist and the country to *assimilate*, and the
process of assimilation, as we have seen in our discussion of abstract art,
requires time and pauses and consolidation. It also frequently involves
a fruitful reaffirmation of more easily understood native traits. The
timetable of this process is unpredictable, for it is established by the
action of artists who work instinctively and spontaneously in one
direction or the other, and it sometimes seems that those who care least
for theory make the determining contributions. Our best regionalists
may well turn out to be men like Hopper and Burchfield who do not
call themselves that. Our best abstract painters may be men like
Marin, Davis, and Knaths who are least bound to programs. "It will be

better," said Leo Stein, "for the painter to be great incidentally than to be great on purpose." [10]

It is the virtue of the broader theory of what constitutes American art that it can comprehend all these and a hundred other opposed and dissimilar talents within its definition. It is the virtue of art in a democracy that it can argue or disregard all theories and continue its protean growth in every direction that promises fruitful reflections on man, on nature, and on spirit. Criticism can help to clarify past directions and may venture to predict future ones, but it cannot prescribe them. "In one word art is free here," as Jarves remarked some eighty-five years ago, "as free to surpass all previous art as it is free to remain, if it so inclines, low and common." [11] In regard to the latter, there seems little ground for concern.

# REVOLUTION IN SUBJECT

# the american scene

1. John F. Weir    **The Gun Foundry**
oil, 1867. Courtesy Putnam County Historical Society.

**2. Louis C. Tiffany      Old New York**
oil, c. 1878. Courtesy Brooklyn Museum.

**3. Jerome Myers      A Windy Corner**
oil, 1907. Courtesy Mrs. Mary Egner Malone.

4. George Luks    Hester Street
oil, 1905. Courtesy Brooklyn Museum.

5. John Sloan    The Haymarket
oil, 1907. Courtesy Brooklyn Museum.

**6. Glenn O. Coleman    Street Bathers**
crayon drawing. Courtesy Whitney Museum of American Art.

**7. Eugene Higgins    Weary**
oil, 1905. Courtesy Kleemann Gallery.

**8. Abastenia St. Leger Eberle    Roller Skating**
bronze, before 1910. Courtesy Whitney Museum of American Art.

**9. Charles Haag    The Strikers**
bronze, c. 1905. Courtesy the Lloyd family.

**10. Isaac Soyer    Employment Agency**
oil, 1937. Courtesy Whitney Museum of American Art.

**11. Reginald Marsh    The Bowl**
tempera, 1933. Courtesy Brooklyn Museum.

**12. William Gropper    The Senate**
oil, 1935. Courtesy Museum of Modern Art, Gift of A. Conger Goodyear.

**13. Fletcher Martin    Out at Home**
oil, 1940. Courtesy Associated American Artists.

**14. Aaron Bohrod     Landscape near Chicago**
oil, 1934. Courtesy Whitney Museum of American Art.

**15. John Steuart Curry     Baptism in Kansas**
oil, 1928. Courtesy Whitney Museum of American Art.

# the machine and
# the subconscious

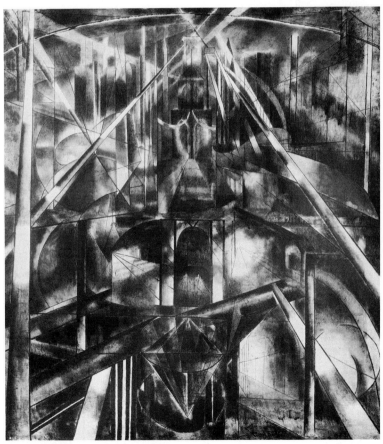

16.  Joseph Stella      Brooklyn Bridge
oil, 1917–18. Courtesy Yale University Art Gallery, Collection Société Anonyme.

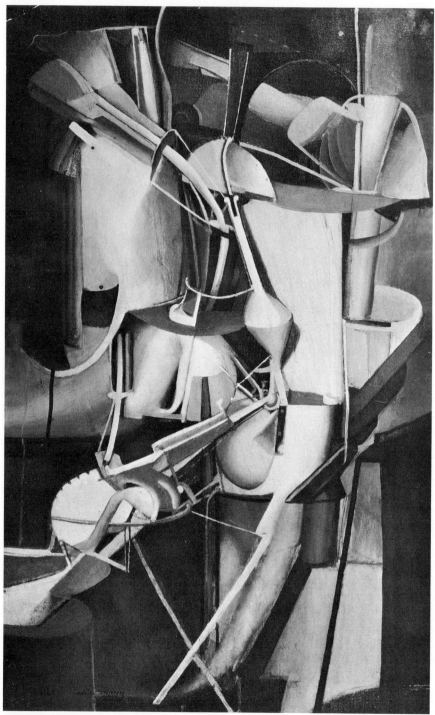

**17. Marcel Duchamp   The Bride**
oil, 1912. Courtesy Philadelphia Museum of Art, Louise and Walter Arensberg Collection.

**18. Francis Picabia
A Young American Girl
in a State of Nudity**
illustration in 291. Courtesy
Museum of Modern Art.

**19. Man Ray    Clock Wheels**
rayograph, 1925. Courtesy Yale University Art Gallery, Collection Société Anonyme.

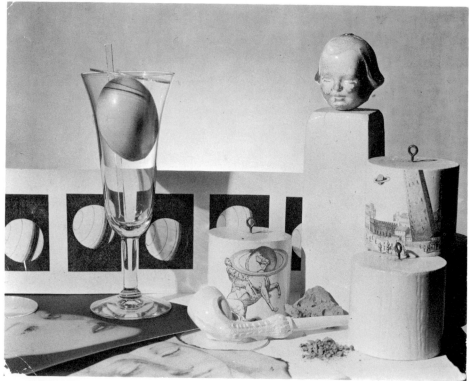

**20. Joseph Cornell    Soap Bubble Set**
arrangement of contents with additional effects, 1936. Courtesy Wadsworth Atheneum.

**21. Federico Castellon    The Dark Figure**
oil, 1938. Courtesy Whitney Museum of American Art.

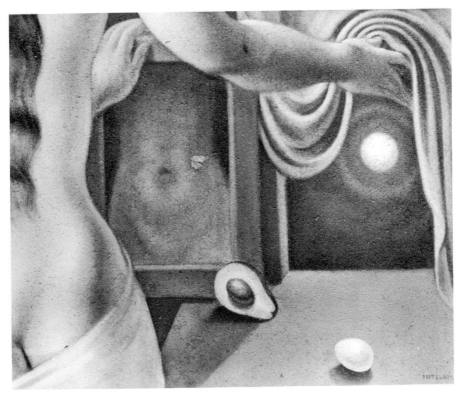

**22. Lorser Feitelson    Genesis, First Version**
oil, 1934. Courtesy San Francisco Museum of Art.

**23. Peter Blume    Key West Beach**
oil, 1940. Courtesy James Thrall Soby.

24. Salvador Dali
Apparition of Face and
Fruit Dish on a Beach
oil, 1938. Courtesy
Wadsworth Atheneum.

25. Dorothea Tanning    Palaestra
oil, 1949. Courtesy the artist.

**26. Matta   The Hanged One**
oil, 1942. Courtesy Museum
of Modern Art.

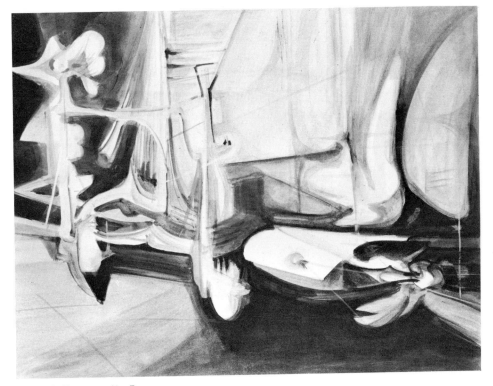

**27. Boris Margo      No. 7**
water color, 1945. Courtesy Betty Parsons Gallery.

**28. Alton Pickens    The Acrobat**
oil, 1947. Courtesy Curt Valentin.

# expressionism

29. Max Weber    Decoration with Cloud
oil, 1913. Courtesy the artist.

**30. Bernard Karfiol      Boy Bathers**
oil, 1916. Courtesy Downtown Gallery.

**31. Alfred H. Maurer      Landscape**
oil, c. 1912. Courtesy Weyhe Gallery.

**32. Charles Demuth      Illustration No. 4 for
Henry James' Turn of the Screw**
water color, 1918. Courtesy Mrs. Frank C. Osborn.

**33. Ben Benn      Mother and Child**
oil, 1915. Courtesy Whitney Museum of American Art.

**34. Lyonel Feininger      Street in Paris**
oil, 1909. Courtesy Buchholz Gallery.

35. Max Weber    Gesture
oil, 1921. Courtesy Mr. and Mrs. F. H. Hirschland.

36. Marsden Hartley    Last of New England — the Beginning of New Mexico
oil, 1918. Courtesy Art Institute of Chicago.

**37. Thomas H. Benton    Chilmark**
oil, 1916. Owner unknown.

38. **Yasuo Kuniyoshi**
**Dream**
ink and wash drawing, 1922.
Courtesy Downtown Gallery.

39. **Ben Shahn**
**The Passion of Sacco and Vanzetti**
tempera, 1931–32. Courtesy
Whitney Museum of American Art.

**40. George Grosz**
**Street Scene**
water color, c. 1934. Courtesy
Associated American Artists.

**41. Philip Evergood**
**Lily and the Sparrows**
oil, 1939. Courtesy
Whitney Museum of American Art.

**42. Max Weber    Hasidic Dance**
oil, 1940. Courtesy Mr. and Mrs. Milton Lowenthal.

**43. Yasuo Kuniyoshi**
**Headless Horse Who Wants to Jump**
oil, 1945. Courtesy Museum of
the Cranbrook Academy of Art.

44. **Franklin C. Watkins** **Dr. George Kamperman**
oil, 1946. Courtesy Dr. and Mrs. George Kamperman.

45. **Alfred H. Maurer** **Self-Portrait with Hat,** oil, 1928. Courtesy Walker Art Center

46. **Abraham Rattner**
**The Emperor**
oil, 1944. Courtesy
Whitney Museum of American Art.

**47. George Grosz    The Pit**
oil, 1946. Courtesy Roland P. Murdock Collection, Wichita Art Museum.

**48. Marsden Hartley    The Lighthouse**
oil, 1940–41. Courtesy William A. M. Burden.

**49. Karl Zerbe    Aging Harlequin**
encaustic, 1946. Courtesy Dr. and Mrs. Michael Watter.

50. Jack Levine    Welcome Home
oil, 1946. Courtesy Brooklyn Museum.

51. Rico Lebrun
Shell of Mary
casein, c. 1949. Courtesy
Jacques Seligmann Gallery.

52. **Hyman Bloom    Buried Treasure**
oil, 1948. Courtesy Durlacher Brothers.

**53.  David Aronson**
**Coronation of the Virgin**
encaustic, 1945. Courtesy
Virginia Museum of Fine Arts.

**54. Minna Harkavy    Leo Stein**
bronze, 1932. Courtesy Midtown Galleries.

**55. Charles Umlauf    Head of Saint**
aluminum, 1949. Courtesy Mortimer Levitt Gallery.

# REVOLUTION IN FORM

# abstract art,
## 1910-1930

56. Max Weber    The Visit
oil, 1919. Courtesy Mr. and Mrs. Milton Lowenthal.

**57. Patrick Henry Bruce    Composition II**
oil, before 1919. Courtesy Yale University Art Gallery, Collection Société Anonyme.

**58.  Morgan Russell    Synchromy No. 5**
oil, 1914. Courtesy Pinakotheka
(Rose Fried) Gallery.

**59. Stanton Macdonald-Wright    Airplane Synchromy in Yellow-Orange**
oil, 1917. Courtesy Metropolitan Museum of Art.

**60. Joseph Stella    Battle of Lights, Coney Island**
oil, 1913. Courtesy Yale University Art Gallery, Collection Société Anonyme.

**61. John Marin    Woolworth Building**
water color, 1915. Courtesy Downtown Gallery.

**62. Robert Delaunay    Eiffel Tower**
ink drawing, 1910. Courtesy Museum of Modern Art,
Purchase Fund.

**63. Lyonel Feininger    The Side Wheeler**
oil, 1913. Courtesy Detroit Institute of Arts.

**64. Arthur G. Dove    Nature Symbolized, No. 2**
pastel, 1911. Courtesy Art Institute of Chicago.

**65.  John R. Covert    Brass Band**
oil and string, 1919. Courtesy Yale University Art
Gallery, Collection Société Anonyme.

**66.  Marsden Hartley**
**Portrait of a German Officer**
oil, 1914. Courtesy Metropolitan
Museum of Art.

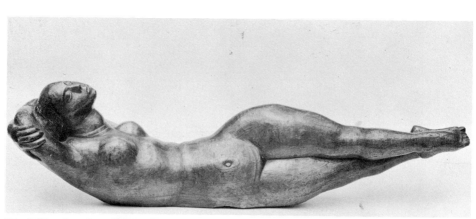

**67. William Zorach    Floating Figure**
African mahogany, 1922. Courtesy Albright Art Gallery, Room of Contemporary Art.

**68. Robert Laurent    Head**
alabaster, 1919. Courtesy
Miss Dorothy Ainsworth.

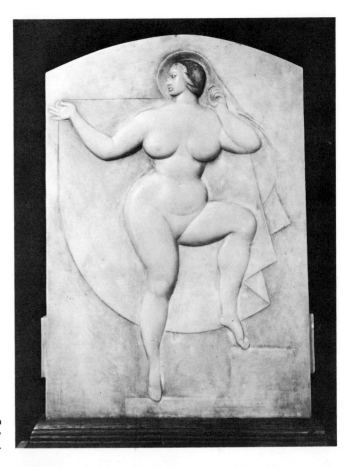

**69. Gaston Lachaise    Woman**
marble, 1918. Courtesy
M. Knoedler and Co.

**70. Elie Nadelman    Horse**
plaster, c. 1914. Courtesy
Mme. Helena Rubinstein.

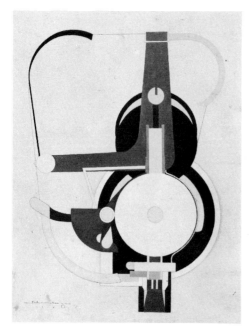

71. Morton L. Schamberg    Machine
oil, 1916. Courtesy Yale University
Art Gallery, Collection Société Anonyme.

72. Charles Demuth    Paquebot Paris
oil, 1921. Courtesy Columbus Gallery of Fine Arts
Ferdinand Howald Collection.

73. **Charles Sheeler**     **Church Street El**
oil, 1922. Courtesy Mrs. Earle Horter.

74. **Charles Sheeler**     **Upper Deck**
oil, 1929. Courtesy Fogg Museum of Art.

**75. Preston Dickinson     The Factory**
oil, c. 1918. Courtesy Museum of Fine Arts, Boston.

**76.  Georgia O'Keeffe
Corn, Dark**
oil, 1924. Courtesy
Metropolitan Museum of Art.

**77.  Niles Spencer
Near Avenue A**
oil, 1933. Courtesy
Museum of Modern Art
Gift of Nelson A. Rockefeller.

**78.  John Marin     Sunset, Casco Bay**
water color, 1919. Courtesy Miss Georgia O'Keeffe.

**79.  Joseph Stella     The Port**
**from New York Interpreted**
oil, 1920–22. Courtesy Newark Museum.

**80. Arthur G. Dove     Goin' Fishin'**
collage, 1925. Courtesy Phillips Gallery.

**81. Stuart Davis     Summer Landscape**
oil, 1930. Courtesy Museum of Modern Art.

# abstract art today

**82. Charles Sheeler      Incantation**
oil, 1946. Courtesy Brooklyn Museum.

83. Bradley Walker Tomlin
Burial, oil, 1943. Courtesy
Metropolitan Museum of Art.

84. Balcomb Greene
The Ancient Form
oil, 1940. Courtesy
Museum of Modern Art.

85. I. Rice Pereira
Transversion
oil and ceramic fluid on
three panes of glass, 1946.
Courtesy Phillips Gallery.

**86. Lyonel Feininger**
**Windclouds at Sundown**
water color, 1948.
Courtesy Buchholz Gallery.

**87. Karl Knaths**
**Duck Flight**
oil, 1948. Courtesy
Whitney Museum of American Art.

**88. Stuart Davis**
**Ultra-Marine**
oil, 1942. Courtesy
Downtown Gallery.

**89. Alexander Calder    Red Palette**
mobile, 1947. Courtesy Buchholz Gallery.

**90. Carl Holty    Suspension of Forms**
oil, 1941. Courtesy Miss Charmion Wiegand.

**91. Arshile Gorky**
**Agony**, oil, 1947. Courtesy
Museum of Modern Art
A. Conger Goodyear Fund.

**92. William Baziotes     The Dwarf**
oil, 1947. Courtesy Museum of Modern Art
A. Conger Goodyear Fund.

**93. Jackson Pollock      No. 10 — 1950**
oil, 1950. Courtesy Mrs. Richard Deutsch.

**94. Mark Rothko**
**Vessels of Magic**
water color, c. 1947. Courtesy
Brooklyn Museum.

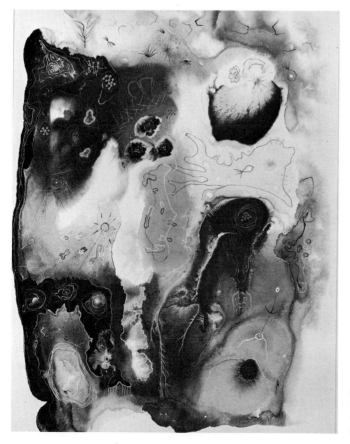

**95. Lawrence Kupferman**
**Invention on a Microscopic Theme**
water color, c. 1949. Courtesy
Brooklyn Museum.

96. Arthur G. Dove     Flour Mill Abstraction No. 2
oil, 1938. Courtesy Phillips Gallery.

97. Theodoros Stamos     Sounds in the Rock
oil, 1946. Courtesy Museum of Modern Art
Gift of Edward W. Root.

**98. Robert Motherwell    Five in the Afternoon**
oil, 1950. Courtesy Kootz Gallery.

**99. Max Weber    Three Literary Gentlemen**
oil, 1945. Courtesy A. P. Rosenberg and Co.

**100.** John Marin    Grey Rock, Blue Grey Sea and Boat
water color, 1938. Courtesy Downtown Gallery.

**101.** William de Kooning    Painting
oil and enamel, 1948. Courtesy Museum of Modern Art, Purchase Fund.

**102. José de Creeft    Maya**
Belgian black granite, c. 1935. Courtesy
Roland P. Murdock Collection
Wichita Art Museum.

**103. John B. Flannagan    Little Creature**
stone, 1941. Courtesy Edgar J. Kaufmann.

**104.** Alexander Archipenko    **Madonna**
marble, 1932. Courtesy a private collector.

**105.** Chaim Gross    **Balancing**
lignum vitae, 1938. Courtesy the artist.

**106. David Smith    The Royal Incubator**
steel-bronze, 1950. Courtesy Willard Gallery.

**107. Theodore J. Roszak**
**Thorn-Blossom** steel and brazed nickel,
1947–48. Courtesy
Whitney Museum of American Art.

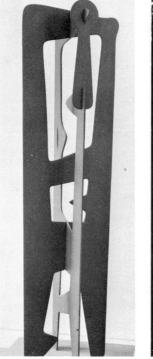

108. **Isamu Noguchi     Construction in Slate**, black slate,
1945. Courtesy Egan Gallery.

109. **Richard Lippold     Variation No. 7 — Full Moon**
nickel chromium and steel wire and brass rods, 1949–50.
Courtesy Museum of Modern Art, Purchase Fund.

110. **Hugo Robus     Girl Washing Her Hair**
marble, 1933. Courtesy Museum of Modern Art
Mrs. John D. Rockefeller Jr. Purchase Fund.

# impressionism and
# romantic realism

111.  Frank Duveneck      The Music Master
oil, 1879. Courtesy Mr. and Mrs. Charles F. Williams.

113. John Sloan    Fifth Avenue Critics
etching, 1905. Courtesy
Whitney Museum of American Art.

112. John Sloan    Hairdresser's Window
oil, 1907. Courtesy Wadsworth Atheneum.

114. William J. Glackens    Park on the River
oil, 1905. Courtesy Brooklyn Museum.

115. Everett Shinn    Illustration for Paul de
Kock's Frédérique, charcoal drawing, c. 1907.
Courtesy Brooklyn Museum.

116. George Luks    The Little Madonna
oil, 1907. Courtesy Addison Gallery
of American Art.

117. George Bellows    Both Members of this Club
oil, 1909. Courtesy National Gallery of Art, Gift of Chester Dale.

**118. John H. Twachtman      Reflections**
oil. Courtesy Brooklyn Museum.

**119.  Maurice Prendergast      April Snow**
oil, 1907. Courtesy Phillips Gallery.

**120.  Arnold Friedman      Forest City**
oil, 1945. Courtesy Marquié Gallery.

121. Eugene Speicher    Greek Boy
oil, 1909. Courtesy the artist.

122. Guy Pène du Bois
A Window in the Union Club
oil, 1919. Courtesy a private collector
through University Gallery
University of Minnesota.

123. Leon Kroll    In the Country
oil, 1916. Courtesy Detroit Institute of Arts.

**124.  George Bellows     Aunt Fanny**
oil, 1920. Courtesy Des Moines Art Center, Edmundson Collection.

**125.  Winslow Homer     Early Morning after a Storm at Sea**
oil, 1902. Courtesy Cleveland Museum of Art
Purchase from J. H. Wade Fund.

126. **Thomas Eakins**
**Addie**, oil, c. 1900.
Courtesy Philadelphia Museum of Art.

127. **Rockwell Kent**    **Toilers of the Sea**
oil, 1907. Courtesy Art Museum of the New Britain Institute.

**128.** Henry Lee McFee **Still Life**, oil, 1916. Courtesy Columbus Gallery of Fine Art, Ferdinand Howald Collection.

**129.** Henry Lee McFee
**Still Life with Decanter**
oil, 1930. Courtesy David C. Allison.

**130.** Maurice Sterne **Resting at the Bazaar** oil, 1912. Courtesy Museum of Modern Art Mrs. John D. Rockefeller, Jr. Purchase Fund.

**131.** Maurice Sterne **Breadmakers** oil, 1923. Courtesy Museum of Fine Arts, Boston.

**132. Walt Kuhn    The Blue Clown**
oil, 1931. Courtesy Whitney Museum of
American Art.

**133. Eugene Speicher    Lilya**
oil, 1930. Courtesy Cincinnati Art Museum.

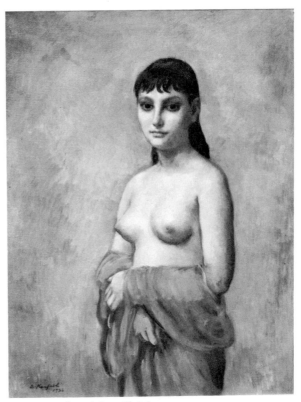

**134. Bernard Karfiol    Christina**
oil, 1936. Courtesy Carnegie Institute.

**135. Julian Levi    Ship Graveyard**
gouache, 1941. Courtesy Philip Loeb.

**136. Isabel Bishop    Waiting**
oil and tempera, 1938. Courtesy
Newark Museum.

**137. Reginald Marsh    Eyes Tested**
wash drawing, 1944. Courtesy Frank K. M.
Rehn Gallery.

**138. Alexander Brook    Summer Wind**
oil, c. 1933. Courtesy Mr. and Mrs. Otto L. Spaeth.

**139. Raphael Soyer    Office Girls**
oil, 1936. Courtesy Whitney Museum of American Art.

**140. Henry Varnum Poor    The Pink Table Cloth**
oil, 1933. Courtesy Cleveland Museum of Art, Purchase for Hinman B. Hurlbut
Collection.

**141. Henry Mattson    Green Seas**
oil, 1938. Courtesy Brooklyn Museum.

**142. Thomas H. Benton    Louisiana Rice Fields**
tempera and oil, 1928. Courtesy Brooklyn Museum.

**143. John Steuart Curry    Hogs Killing Rattlesnake**
oil, 1930. Courtesy Art Institute of Chicago.

144. **Charles Burchfield    House of Mystery**
tempera and oil, 1924. Courtesy Art Institute of Chicago.

**145. Edward Hopper    Night Hawks**
oil, 1942. Courtesy Art Institute of Chicago.

**146. Edward Hopper    Dawn in Pennsylvania**
oil, 1942. Courtesy Mr. and Mrs. Otto L. Spaeth.

147. Oronzio Maldarelli     Beatrice
marble, 1948. Courtesy Midtown Galleries.

148. Mahonri Young     The Organ Grinder
bronze, c. 1911. Courtesy Kraushaar Galleries.

149. Heinz Warneke
Bear Cub
stone, c. 1929. Courtesy the artist.

**150. William Zorach    Victory**
French marble, 1945. Courtesy Downtown Gallery.

**151. Robert Laurent    Seated Nude**
alabaster, 1940. Courtesy Kraushaar Galleries.

152. **Zoltan Sepeshy** **Driftwood**
tempera, 1943. Courtesy Midtown Galleries.

153. **Joseph Hirsch** **The Confidence**
oil, 1941. Courtesy Samuel Spewack.

# realists and primitives

**154.** **John F. Peto**    **Still Life with Lanterns**
oil, after 1889. Courtesy Brooklyn Museum.

**155. William M. Harnett      Emblems of Peace**
oil, 1890. Courtesy Springfield Museum of Fine Arts.

**156. Walter Tandy Murch      The Circle**
oil, c. 1948. Courtesy Brooklyn Museum.

**157. Frank Califano**
**Evening Usualty**
oil, before 1925. Owner unknown.

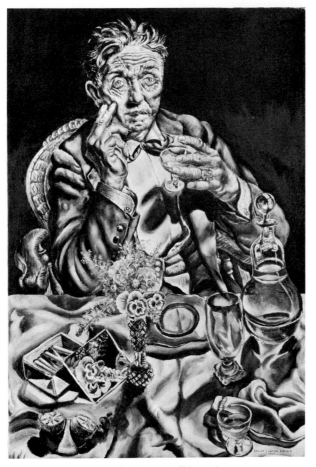

**158. Ivan Le Lorraine Albright    Self-Portrait**
oil, 1935. Courtesy Earle Ludgin.

159. Martin J. Heade    Spring Shower
Connecticut Valley, oil, 1868.
Courtesy Museum of Fine Arts, Boston
M. and M. Karolik Collection.

160. Charles Herbert Moore
The Old Bridge  oil, 1868.
Courtesy Art Museum,
Princeton University.

161. Edward Bruce    A Landscape of Provence
oil, 1928. Courtesy Mrs. Harlan Stone.

**162. Andrew Wyeth    Christina's World**
tempera, 1948. Courtesy Museum of Modern Art, Purchase Fund.

**163. Peter Hurd    The Rainy Season**
tempera, 1940. Courtesy Brooklyn Museum.

**164. Edmund Lewandowski    Industrial Composition**
water color, 1939. Courtesy Brooklyn Museum.

**165. Charles Sheeler    City Interior**
oil, 1936. Courtesy Worcester Art Museum.

**166. Theodore Lux Feininger**
**Ghosts of Engines**
oil, 1946. Courtesy Museum of Modern Art
Gift of Griffis Foundation.

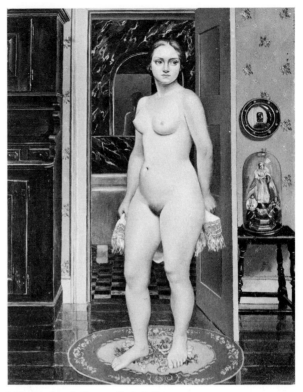

**167. Audrey Buller    Nude in Doorway**
oil, 1933. Courtesy the artist.

**168. Alexandre Hogue    Dust Bowl**
oil, before 1940. Courtesy Permanent Collection, Fine Arts Department
International Business Machines Corp.

**169. Grant Wood    American Gothic**
oil, 1930. Courtesy Art Institute of Chicago.

**170. Henry Koerner    Monkey Bars**
oil, 1947. Courtesy Mr. and Mrs. Robert Sherry.

**171. O. Louis Guglielmi    Terror in Brooklyn**
oil, 1941. Courtesy Whitney Museum of American Art.

**172. Paul Cadmus    Playground**
oil, 1948. Courtesy Midtown Galleries.

173. Peter Blume    The Rock
oil, 1944–48. Courtesy Edgar J. Kaufmann, Jr.

174.  Honore Sharrer
The Industrial Scene
center panel of
Tribute to the American Working People
oil, 1945–50. Courtesy M. Knoedler and Co.

**175. Ben Shahn    Father and Child**
tempera, 1946. Courtesy James Thrall Soby.

**176. Joseph Pickett**
**Manchester Valley**
oil, 1914–18? Courtesy
Museum of Modern Art
Gift of Mrs. John D. Rockefeller, Jr.

**177. John Kane**
**Self-Portrait**
oil, 1929. Courtesy Museum of Modern Art
Mrs. John D. Rockefeller Jr. Purchase Fund.

**178. Morris Hirshfield** **Tiger,** oil, 1940.
Courtesy Museum of Modern Art
Mrs. John D. Rockefeller, Jr. Purchase Fund.

# romantic visionaries

**179. Albert P. Ryder    The Flying Dutchman**
oil, c. 1887. Courtesy National Collection of Fine Arts
Smithsonian Institute.

**180. Albert P. Ryder      Forest of Arden**
oil, 1897. Courtesy Stephen C. Clark.

**181. Benjamin Kopman      Meditation**
oil, 1914. Courtesy Mrs. Frederic Fairchild Sherman.

**182. Arthur B. Davies    Crescendo**
oil, 1910. Courtesy Whitney Museum of American Art.

**183. Middleton Manigault    Source**
oil, c. 1914. Courtesy Estate of Mary H. Rumsey.

**184. Louis M. Eilshemius    Afternoon Wind**
oil, 1899. Courtesy Museum of Modern Art.

185. Raymond Breinin
They Guard in the Night
oil, 1945. Courtesy Paul Baron.

186. John Carroll
White Lace
oil, 1935. Courtesy Toledo Museum of Art.

187. Hobson Pittman
The Widow
oil, 1938. Courtesy
Whitney Museum of American Art.

188. Charles Burchfield
Night Wind
water color, 1918
Courtesy A. Conger Goodyear.

189. Charles Burchfield
Clatter of Crows in a Spring Woods
water color, 1949
Courtesy Frank K. M. Rehn Gallery.

190. Oscar Bluemner
Moonshine Fantasy
oil, before 1930. Owner unknown.

191. Arthur G. Dove     Gold, Green and Brown
oil, 1940. Courtesy Phillips Gallery.

**192. Elliot Orr
The Storm**
oil, 1940. Courtesy Brooklyn Museum.

**193. Matthew Barnes     High Peak**
oil, 1936. Courtesy Museum of Modern Art
acquired through Lillie P. Bliss Bequest.

**194. Kenneth Callahan    Conversation**
water color, 1944–45. Courtesy Brooklyn Museum.

**195. C. S. Price    The Fisherman**
oil, 1941. Courtesy Detroit Institute of Arts.

**196. Mark Tobey    Tundra**
tempera, 1944. Courtesy Willard Gallery.

**197. Morris Graves    Bird Singing in the Moonlight**
gouache, 1938–39. Courtesy Museum of Modern Art.

**198. Darrel Austin    Moon Song**
oil, 1942. Courtesy Edward A. Bragaline.

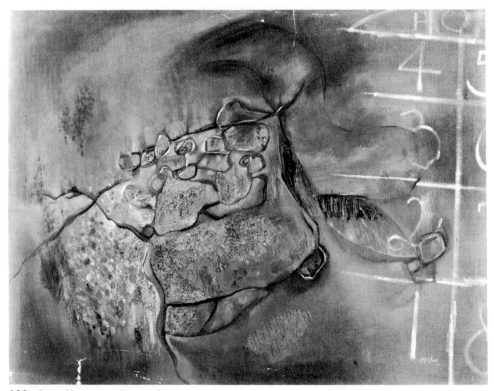

**199. Loren MacIver    Hopscotch**
oil, 1940. Courtesy Museum of Modern Art, Purchase Fund.

# notes

# NOTES

## 1. a survey

1. Irene Sargent, "The Wavy Line," *Craftsman*, 2:133, 135 (1902). Benjamin De Casseres, "Caricature and New York," *Camera Work*, 26:17 (1909). Ralph Davol, "Early American Artists," *New England Magazine*, n.s., 45:479 (1912).

2. Davies' statement was also printed in the Catalogue of the International Exhibition of Modern Art, as the show was officially called.

3. Royal Cortissoz, *Century*, 85:815 (1913). W. D. MacColl, *Forum*, 50:24 (1913). Guy Pène du Bois, *Arts and Decoration*, 3:151 (1913).

4. "Art in New York This Season," *Craftsman*, 24:134 (1913). New York, Whitney Museum of American Art, Pioneers of Modern Art in America Exhibition (1946), Catalogue; Lloyd Goodrich's introduction gives the best summary of the organization and course of the Armory Show.

## 2. the american scene

1. New York *Evening Post*, April 27, 1893.

2. Bliss Carman, "The Leaven of Art," *Craftsman*, 12:152 (1907).

3. "Thoughts on Art," *Dial*, 1:372 (1841). Birge Harrison, *Landscape Painting* (New York: Scribner's, 1910), pp. 98, 229–30. Asher B. Durand, *Crayon*, 1:275 (1855).

4. W. Mackay Laffan, "The Material of American Landscape," *American Art Review*, 1:23 (1880).

5. Charles W. Larned, "The Spirit of Art," *Studio*, 1:146 (1883).

6. Richmond, Virginia Museum of Fine Arts, Jerome Myers Memorial Exhibition (1942), Catalogue, p. 9.

7. Charles W. Barrell, "The Real Drama of the Slums," *Craftsman*, 15:559 (1909). Giles Edgerton, "Is America Selling Her Birthright in Art for a Mess of Pottage?" *Craftsman*, 11:657 (1907); 14:120 (1908).

8. Arnold Friedman, "The Original Independent Show, 1908," MS. in the collection of the Museum of Modern Art. *Craftsman*, 14:345 (1908).

9. Louis H. Sullivan, "Is Our Art a Betrayal Rather Than an Expression of American Life?" *Craftsman*, 15:403 (1909). William L. Price, "Is American Art Captive to the Dead Past?" *Craftsman*, 15:515 (1909).

10. *Ibid.*, 516.

11. Claggett Wilson in "Symposium," *Creative Art*, 2:xl (April 1928).

12. Forbes Watson, "Charles Sheeler," *Arts*, 3:335 (1923). Virgil Barker, "The Water Colors of John Marin," *Arts*, 5:65 (1924). Leo Stein, "Art and Common Sense," *New Republic*, 11:13 (1917). Oliver S. Tonks, "The Creed of Abstract Art," *Arts*, 7:215 (1925).

13. Thomas Craven, "Politics and the Painting Business," *American Mercury*, 27:463 (1932); "Our Art Becomes American," *Harper's Magazine*, 171:430, 434, 436, 437 (1935).

## 3. the machine and the subconscious

1. Samuel Atkins Eliot, "The Present and Future of American Art," *North American Review*, 83:91 (1856).

2. MS. in the collection of the Whitney Museum of American Art.

3. Alfred H. Barr, Jr., and Georges Hugnet, *Fantastic Art, Dada, Surrealism*, 2nd ed. (New York: Museum of Modern Art, 1937), p. 15.

4. Van Wyck Brooks, *The Ordeal of Mark Twain* (New York: Dutton, 1920; copyright, 1948, Van Wyck Brooks).

5. Benjamin De Casseres, "Insincerity: A New Vice," *Camera Work*, 42:17 (1913).

Marius de Zayas, "The Sun Has Set," *Camera Work*, 39:17 (1912).

6. *Camera Work*, special number, p. 57 (June 1913).

7. *Arts*, 1:64 (1921).

8. Charles Burchfield, "On the Middle Border," *Creative Art*, 3:xxv (September 1928).

9. Barr and Hugnet, pp. 11, 60.

10. Edouard Roditi, "William Harnett: American Necromantic," *View*, p. 9 (November 1945).

11. Benjamin De Casseres, "The Unconscious in Art" and "Modernity and the Decadence," *Camera Work*, 36:17 (1911), 37:17 (1912).

12. Alfred Stieglitz, "One Hour's Sleep — Three Dreams," *291*, first issue (March 1915).

13. Max Ernst, *Beyond Painting*, Documents of Modern Art series, vol. VII (New York: Wittenborn, Schultz, 1948), p. vi.

14. New York, Museum of Modern Art, Fourteen Americans Exhibition (1946), Catalogue, p. 49.

## 4. expressionism

1. *Craftsman*, 14:342 (1908).

2. Charles H. Caffin, "Henri Matisse and Isadora Duncan," *Camera Work*, 25:17 (1909). Gelett Burgess, "The Wild Men of Paris," *Architectural Record*, 27:401 (1910).

3. Letter to the author.

4. Chicago, Art Institute, Arthur Jerome Eddy Collection of Modern Paintings and Sculpture, Catalogue (undated), no. 1; compare Bloch painting illustrated with the earlier Kandinsky, "Entwurf zu Komposition Nr. 4," illustrated in the latter's *Der Blaue Reiter* (1912), opp. p. 64.

5. Lloyd Goodrich, *Max Weber* (Macmillan, 1949), p. 40.

6. Marsden Hartley, "Art — And the Personal Life," *Creative Art*, 3:xxxi (June 1928).

7. New York, Forum Exhibition of Modern American Painters (1916), Catalogue.

8. Lloyd Goodrich, *Yasuo Kuniyoshi* (Macmillan, 1948), p. 23.

9. *William Gropper*, with preface by Philip Evergood (New York: A. C. A. Galleries, 1944).

10. Fourteen Americans Exhibition, Catalogue, p. 11.

## 5. abstract art, 1910–1930

1. New York, Museum of Modern Art, Cubism and Abstract Art Exhibition (1936), Catalogue, p. 19.

2. Letter from Suzanne Mullet Smith to the Whitney Museum of American Art. I have not seen the picture, which is in the Dove collection.

3. Henry L. McFee, "My Painting and its Development," *Creative Art*, 4:xxiv (March 1929).

4. Arthur Jerome Eddy, *Cubists and Post-Impressionism* (1914), p. 89. John Weichsel, "Cosmism or Amorphism," *Camera Work*, 42–43:81–82 (1913).

5. Paris, Bernheim-jeune et cie., Synchromist Exhibition (1913), Catalogue.

6. Willard Huntington Wright, "Impressionism to Synchromism," *Forum*, 50:757ff. (1913).

7. *Ibid*.

8. McFee, "My Painting."

9. Letter to the author. It has since been discovered that Bruce destroyed all but fifteen of his later works. Several of these were exhibited in November 1950 at the Pinakotheka Gallery in New York.

10. See Walter Pach, "Some Reflections on Modern Art Suggested by the Career of Arthur Burdett Frost, Jr.," *Scribner's*, 63:637 (1918).

11. New York, Museum of Modern Art, Feininger-Hartley Exhibition (1944), Catalogue, p. 11.

12. *Camera Work*, 32:41 (1910).

13. Andrew Dasburg, "Cubism — Its Rise and Influence," *Arts*, 4:279 (1923).

14. William Zorach, "New Tendencies in Art," *Arts*, 2:13 (October 1921).

15. Horace Brodzky, "Concerning Sculpture and Robert Laurent," *Arts*, 1:13 (May 1921).

16. Katherine S. Dreier, *David Burliuk* (New York: Wittenborn, Schultz, 1944), p. 143.

17. Dasburg, p. 282.

18. Leo Stein, "Tradition and Art," *Arts*, 7:265 (1925).

## 6. abstract art today

1. James Johnson Sweeney, *Stuart Davis* (New York: Museum of Modern Art, 1945), p. 29.
2. New York, New Art Circle, Benjamin Kopman Exhibition (1935), Catalogue. Stanton Macdonald-Wright, "Blueprint for a Textbook on Art," *College Art Journal*, 4:144 (1945).
3. Chicago, Art Institute, Abstract and Surrealist American Art Exhibition (1947–48).
4. *Magazine of Art*, 42:92 (1949).
5. New York, Julien Levy Gallery, Arshile Gorky Exhibition (1945).
6. Fourteen Americans Exhibition, Catalogue, p. 36.
7. Sidney Janis, *Abstract and Surrealist Art in America* (New York: Harcourt, Brace, 1944), p. 65.
8. John Marin, "John Marin by Himself," *Creative Art*, 3:xxxvi–xxxvii (October 1928).
9. John B. Flannagan, "The Image in the Rock," *Magazine of Art*, 35:95 (1942).
10. *Tiger's Eye*, 1:76 (June 1948).
11. Fourteen Americans Exhibition, Catalogue, p. 59.

## 7. romantic realism and impressionism

1. Sadakichi Hartmann, *A History of American Art* (Boston: L. C. Page, 1902), II, 278–279. This and subsequent quotations by permission of the publisher. F. J. Mather, "The Independent Artists," *Nation*, 90:361 (1910). J. N. Laurvik, "New Tendencies in Art," *Camera Work*, 22:33 (1908). Robert Henri, "Progress in Our National Art," *Craftsman*, 15:387 (1909).
2. Friedman, "The Original Independent Show."
3. Pioneers of Modern Art in America Exhibition, Catalogue, p. 6.
4. New York, Kevorkian Gallery, Henry Varnum Poor Exhibition (1920), Catalogue.
5. *Art Digest*, 9:29 (September 1, 1935).
6. James Thrall Soby and Dorothy C. Miller, *Romantic Painting in America*, (New York: Museum of Modern Art, 1943), p. 39. Soby, *Contemporary Painters* (Museum of Modern Art, 1948), and Lloyd Goodrich, *Edward Hopper* (Penguin Books, 1949), are two quite different but equally sensitive analyses of Hopper's work.
7. Parker Tyler, "Edward Hopper: Alienation by Light," *Magazine of Art*, 41:290 (1948).
8. Selene A. Armstrong, "Solon Borglum: Sculptor of American Life," *Craftsman*, 12:382 (1907).
9. Allen Tucker, "My Friend's Friend," *Arts*, 5:156 (1924).

## 8. realists and primitives

1. *Art Union*, 1:42–43 (1884).
2. Ralph Waldo Emerson, *Nature* (1836). Clara Barrus, *The Heart of Burroughs' Journals* (1928), p. 92, entry of September 1, 1882. Emerson, "Art," *Essays*, first series (1844).
3. New York, Museum of Modern Art, American Realists and Magic Realists Exhibition (1943), Catalogue, p. 5.
4. Alfred Frankenstein, "Harnett, True and False," *Art Bulletin*, 31:38–56 (1949); "Harnett: One Century," *Art News*, 47:14–17, 52–53 (September 1948).
5. American Realists and Magic Realists Exhibition, Catalogue, p. 25.
6. *Ibid.*, p. 58.
7. *Ibid.*, p. 47.
8. Soby, *Contemporary Painters*, p. 54.
9. Fourteen Americans Exhibition, Catalogue, p. 62.
10. Grace Pagano, *The Encyclopaedia Britannica Collection of Contemporary American Painting* (Encyclopaedia Britannica, 1946).

## 9. romantic visionaries

1. *International Studio*, 61:xc (May 1917).
2. John Spargo, "Van Dearing Perrine," *Craftsman*, 12:489 (1907).
3. Charles Burchfield, "On the Middle Border," *Creative Art*, 3:xxviii (September 1928).
4. See Duncan Phillips, "Arthur G. Dove, 1880–1946," *Magazine of Art*, 40:193 (1947).
5. Soby, *Contemporary Painters*, p. 49.
6. New York, Museum of Modern Art, *Americans 1942 Exhibition* (1942), Catalogue, p. 11.
7. *Fourteen Americans Exhibition*, Catalogue, p. 28.

## 10. the artist in the modern world

1. Henry T. Tuckerman, *Book of the Artists* (1867), pp. 168–169.
2. Benjamin De Casseres, "American Indifference," *Camera Work*, 27:24 (1909).
3. "Remarks on the Progress and Present State of the Fine Arts in the United States," *Analectic Magazine*, 6:368–369 (1815). "Indifference to Art," *Nation*, 75:241 (1902).
4. Claude Phillips, "The Quality of Emotion in Modern Art," *North American Review*, 174:348 (1902).
5. Goodrich, *Max Weber*, p. 19.
6. Friedman, "The Original Independent Show."
7. *Craftsman*, 18:290–291 (1910).
8. *Arts*, 1:34 (May 1921).
9. Hartmann, *A History of American Art*, II, 224.
10. Elizabeth McCausland, "Why Can't America Afford Art?" *Magazine of Art*, 39:18 (1946).

## 11. trends and portents

1. *Pioneers of Modern Art in America Exhibition*, Catalogue, p. 17.
2. Ralph Waldo Emerson, "The Poet," *Essays*, second series (1844).
3. *Studio*, 1:25 (1883).
4. René D'Harnoncourt, "Challenge and Promise: Modern Art and Modern Society," *Magazine of Art*, 41:252 (1948).
5. *Cubism and Abstract Art Exhibition*, Catalogue, p. 200.
6. S. R. Koehler, "The Future of Art," *American Art Review*, 1:32 (1880).
7. D'Harnoncourt, "Challenge and Promise."
8. *Magazine of Art*, 42:82–102 (1949).

## 12. what is american?

1. Jerome Mellquist, *The Emergence of An American Art* (Scribner, 1942).
2. "Remarks on the Progress and Present State of the Fine Arts," *Analectic Magazine*.
3. Birge Harrison, "The Future of American Art," *North American Review*, 189:27 (1909).
4. John A. Kouwenhoven, *Made in America* (New York: Doubleday, 1948).
5. E. P. Richardson, *Washington Allston* (University of Chicago Press, 1948), pp. 136–137. Detroit Institute of Arts and Boston, Museum of Fine Arts, *Washington Allston Exhibition* (1947), Catalogue, p. 5.
6. Frank T. Robinson, "Prize Fund and Society Exhibitions," *American Art Illustrated*, 1:227 (1887). Hartmann, II, 161–162. Kouwenhoven, *Made in America*. Thomas Craven, "Politics & the Painting Business," *American Mercury*, 27:463 (1932); *Art Digest* (quoted from New York *American*), 9:14 (September 1, 1935).
7. James Jackson Jarves, *The Art-Idea* (1864), pp. 197–198.
8. Robert Henri, *The Art Spirit* (1923), p. 126.
9. *Pioneers of Modern Art in America Exhibition*, Catalogue, p. 17.
10. Leo Stein, "Art and Common Sense," *New Republic*, 11:15 (1917).
11. Jarves, p. 197.

# index

# index

**168**